*Tony Grady is a shining example* ... *opportunity, but also the greatest* ... *history and his own story, he mak* ... *and American values triumph over ... ......... of freedom.* Tony also makes a compelling case that what we need now more than ever are men and women of faith and virtue who will restore these values during a time when they are discounted and ridiculed. These values have come under attack and have been eroded before our very eyes, but Tony's story gives us hope that those values and the American dream are not dead. Enjoy Tony's story. It is gripping. Embrace Tony's vision of leadership. It is vital for our survival.*

Dr. Brian Borgman
Founding Pastor of Grace Community Church
Minden, Nevada

Tony's memoir is a call to arms to preserve the American Dream that enabled him to become a top tier test pilot who capped his Air Force career by commanding the B2 Bomber Test Squadron. Tony stands tall (literally and figuratively) in the pantheon of black men raised with Christian principles, that equipped them to survive racism and other forms of adversity and to excel. The Democrat party, founded to preserve and extend slavery and to discriminate against blacks, has become the home for the radical political left that threatens the preservation of the American Dream. It promotes the godless ideologies of Socialism and Marxism rebranded today as Critical Race Theory, DEI (Diversity, Equity, and Inclusion) and Intersectionality. Tony has answered the call to be a soldier in the war against the evil forces that hate America and want to destroy Western Civilization founded on Judeo-Christian principles. His life story shows he is well qualified to make a major impact in preserving the American Dream and can well represent the state of Nevada in the U.S. Senate.

Bill Long, U.S. Air Force veteran,
former IBM Systems Engineer and
founder of Centura Software

An engaging story about an unusual life of an American patriot. A delightful read with interesting vignettes, or mini stories, to illustrate Tony Grady's life.

Patty Cafferata, former Nevada State Treasurer

*An amazing and inspiring story of how leaders of character through perseverance, determination, and hard work overcome adversity, economic and social (racial) barriers to achieve the American Dream! Tony and his family exemplify the very role models we look to, both now and in the future! This is a chronicle of the best of the best of America!*

Charlie Coolidge, Lieutenant General Charlie Coolidge
U.S. Air Force (Retired)

Everyone needs to read *American Values: Another Voice*. Through his life story, Tony Grady obliterates the lies perpetuated by race-baiting America haters. He offers a heavy dose of truth for a lost nation. I have worked with many elected officials, both foreign and domestic, and can tell you Tony Grady's extraordinary intelligence and sound wisdom are rare. Protecting him would be an honor.

Matthew Morgeson
Special Agent
United States Secret Service – Retired

*A candid and honest review of the ethical and constitutional ideals that mold great leaders. This book describes Tony Grady's life journey of service before self and is a testament to family values that created his strength of character, faith, and resilience.... Essential reading for future leaders.*

Major General N. E. Rick Nelson,
U.S. Marine Corps (Retired)

# OTHER PUBLICATIONS BY THE AUTHOR

*The Moral Domain of War: A View From the Cockpit*

*Young Scientist Journeys (Volume 1)*[1]

# AMERICAN VALUES: ANOTHER VOICE

## A Pilot's Perspective on Living the American Dream

*To Carol,*
*Thank you for your support.*
*Tony Grady*
*September 4, 2024*

*Tony Grady*

Copyright © 2023 Tony Grady.

The appearance of U.S. Department of Defense (DoD) visual information does not imply or constitute DoD endorsement.

All Rights Reserved. No portion of this book may be reproduced in any form without permission from the publisher, except as permitted by U.S. copyright law.

*The views and opinions in this book are solely those of the author and do not reflect official sanctioning or endorsement by the Department of the Air Force or any element of the Department of Defense.*

ISBN Paperback: 978-1-960346-20-9
ISBN Ebook: 978-1-960346-21-6

**THE BIG RED**
PUBLISHING

*If I have seen further, it is by standing on the shoulder of giants.*
Isaac Newton, Letter to Robert Hooke, February 5, 1675

To Walter A. Grady Sr. and Dorothy H. Grady
The giants upon whose shoulders I stand.

Tony Grady
September 4, 2023

# TABLE OF CONTENTS

Acknowledgments . . . . . . . . . . . . . . . . . . . . . . . . . . . . . . . . . xi
Foreword . . . . . . . . . . . . . . . . . . . . . . . . . . . . . . . . . . . . . . . . . xv
Introduction . . . . . . . . . . . . . . . . . . . . . . . . . . . . . . . . . . . . . xxi
Chapter 1      Foundation . . . . . . . . . . . . . . . . . . . . . . . . . . . . . 1
Chapter 2      My Flight Path: An Overview . . . . . . . . . . . . . . . . . 22
Chapter 3      Virtue . . . . . . . . . . . . . . . . . . . . . . . . . . . . . . . . . 30
Chapter 4      Strength of Character . . . . . . . . . . . . . . . . . . . . . . 39
Chapter 5      Liberty . . . . . . . . . . . . . . . . . . . . . . . . . . . . . . . . 58
Chapter 6      Faith . . . . . . . . . . . . . . . . . . . . . . . . . . . . . . . . . 70
Chapter 7      The Tribe . . . . . . . . . . . . . . . . . . . . . . . . . . . . . . 93
Chapter 8      Where I Stand . . . . . . . . . . . . . . . . . . . . . . . . . . 108
Chapter 9      The Instruction Manual of Personal Experience . . . . 122
Chapter 10     So What? . . . . . . . . . . . . . . . . . . . . . . . . . . . . . 139
Appendix . . . . . . . . . . . . . . . . . . . . . . . . . . . . . . . . . . . . . . . 153
Endnotes . . . . . . . . . . . . . . . . . . . . . . . . . . . . . . . . . . . . . . . 169
Biography of Lieutenant Colonel
Walter A. "Tony" Grady, Jr., USAF Retired . . . . . . . . . . . . . . . 181
Photos and Illustrations . . . . . . . . . . . . . . . . . . . . . . . . . . . . 185

# ACKNOWLEDGMENTS

Undertaking the task of writing this memoir caused me to dive into the area of self-examination. This was a much more difficult journey than I anticipated. I am glad that I endured the ordeal because I wanted to tell others a story, an important story. This book came about after I campaigned in 2022 to become Nevada's Lieutenant Governor. I had such a great showing as a first-time political candidate, though ultimately, I was unsuccessful in obtaining the office. In the aftermath, I was encouraged to write my story because many were interested in how I became the person that I am. I hope this book will answer that question. However, it would have been impossible to adequately tell the story without those who came alongside me to assist in completing the task of writing this memoir.

I would like to especially thank the following individuals whose contributions benefited me in this endeavor. My friend Rick Vandam, whose expert piloting skills earned him multiple wins in the National Championship Air Races held in Reno, Nevada, along with Fred Telling, the stalwart Chairman and Chief Executive Officer of the Reno Air Race Association, the organization that plans and carries out the races. Fred is also a member of the air race pilot family. They helped me find photos of air race airplanes that I needed on short notice in the midst of busy schedules. Tony Logoteta the Chief Operations Officer of the Reno Air Race Association graciously gave me permission to use the photos of the air race airplanes from their website so that I could include them in this book. Thank you, gentlemen, for enabling me to visually share a world that is most likely foreign to those who will read this book.

Writing requires long hours of editing. I greatly appreciate the efforts of Janis Galassini, Nevada's Washoe County Clerk, who is always ready and willing to serve. She joyfully read through the manuscript and gave me valuable feedback. Thank you, Jan. The husband-and-wife tag team of Ralph and Betty Camp, friends from church and retired missionaries, whose eagle eyes detected many items I missed. These individuals greatly improved the manuscript. Jan, Ralph, and Betty I appreciate your efforts and diligence. I am especially thankful for the art and cover design by Carrie Zeidman, an exceptionally talented graphic artist. Her knack for style brought out the essence of the book that existed in my mind in a way that others might understand and appreciate it. Her refinement of the photographs in this book without question made my ideas come to life. Thank you, Carrie!

I thank my good friend John Reed, a fellow 1977 United States Air Force Academy classmate, for writing the Foreword to this memoir. Our friendship over the years springing from a common college experience, along with our bond as military pilots, who were like fish out of water when the Air Force took us out of the cockpit to serve on the Air Force staff in the Pentagon. This made him the perfect person to set the tone for this memoir. John, your thoughts and insights were extremely helpful. Mark Clodfelter, another Academy classmate, gave me a sorely needed critique of the manuscript which I greatly appreciate because we think very differently. His expertise as a trained historian and published author enabled him to challenge my assertions. Mark, thank you for your candid comments. I appreciate the thoughts and heartfelt stories of friends I met while living in Bangkok, Thailand, Judy Hobbs, Anne Gregory and her brother, Charlie who helped give the missionary kid perspective while growing up overseas. Their parents were missionaries in Thailand. Judy, Anne, and Charlie, I appreciate your willingness to share your memories and reflections. I also thank Al Gilani, Principal of The Big Red Consulting, and his very able program manager Connie Inggs and her team who helped this memoir become a final product for the public to read. Their suggestions were invaluable.

# AMERICAN VALUES: ANOTHER VOICE

The heart of the memoir is the story. Pulling it together would not have been possible without the many hours that my cousins Alice Bell, and Paula Grady-Ferguson, and my sister, Walteen Grady Truely, spent talking with me. Hearing their thoughts were essential to filling many of the gaps in time from my own memory and stories that predated my birth. Thank you, Alice, Paula, and Walteen for your patient endurance. Though he is no longer with us, my Uncle Gordon produced valuable material used to create this memoir by meticulously recording our family history while he was alive. His personal writings were the foundation for this effort, and I thank him for his foresight to preserve the family history for future use. I also am indebted to my wonderful wife of forty years, Donna Grady. Her moral support was precious and essential. She made sure that I ate properly when I lost track of time while writing, and that our home functions continued smoothly while my mind was on the book. I also appreciated her comments on the manuscript as this book progressed. Her encouragement kept me moving along, especially during the difficult times when articulating my thoughts stalled. Thank you, Donna, my love, and my bride for your support through 'for better and for worse.'

The key person in this entire effort, however, was Virginia Starrett. Her fourteen years of instructing college students in the proper use of the English language as an Assistant Professor, her extensive experience in publishing several genres of literature, and serving for ten years as the managing editor of The South Coast Poetry Journal, were essential to this memoir becoming a reality. She took the manuscript, a rough piece of coal, and labored long hours over several months, meeting with me on numerous occasions, giving me assignments to write and rewrite until the manuscript took shape and became a well-honed diamond glistening in the sunlight. Without her efforts this memoir would never have come about. There are no words to adequately thank you, Virginia, for your labor of love that made an idea become a reality. I am grateful for what you enabled me to achieve in completing this memoir. Finally, I give thanks to the Lord Jesus Christ who created me, saved me, and directs my steps. To God be the glory.

# TONY GRADY

I appreciate the efforts of all who helped me complete this memoir. Any errors in this book are solely my responsibility. I hope you enjoy reading it and afterwards have a better understanding of "who is Tony Grady?"

Tony Grady<br>
Reno, Nevada<br>
October 26, 2023

# FOREWORD

**"Man's Flight Through Life is Sustained by the Power of His Knowledge,"** reads the inscription on the Statue, "Eagle and Fledglings" (by Artist Austin "Dusty" Miller, 1958) at the United States Air Force Academy. The statue rests on the Terrazzo, the Academy's common area, linking the dorms, the dining hall, the library, and the academic buildings. The Cadet Chapel towers over the Terrazzo and is distinctly recognizable. The philosophy of the statue resounds with many of the "Long Blue Line," the previous graduates of this august institution. Clearly, the inscription admonishes the graduates to consider education in all its forms a lifelong endeavor. No one exemplifies this philosophy more than Lieutenant Colonel Walter A. "Tony" Grady, Jr, USAF retired. I am excited and honored to introduce you to this Great American and his insightful memoir.

Tony is a very accomplished man, well-grounded by his Christian Faith, his lovely wife of over forty years, Donna, and his unabashed

Tony Grady standing by the Eagle and Fledglings Statue in the Air Gardens at the United States Air Force Academy, Colorado, Springs, Colorado, on May 30, 1977.

love for America. He is, by self-admission, a skeptic. This explains his persistent curiosity and pursuit of the truth; not "his" truth, or "lived experience truth," but THE truth. His search for the truth has led him to conclusions about Faith, Family and America, bolstering his foundation and steadfastness. He observes today's America and dislikes our trajectory. Not content to grouse and complain, he intends to help put our Constitutional Republic back on track.

Tony's upbringing and early development are compelling. However, I wasn't there for that. He'll cover it in the chapters ahead, so I won't. Tony and I began our military transition on July 2, 1973, as proud members of the Class of '77 at the United States Air Force Academy. Besides the challenges of Basic Cadet Training (BCT, affectionately known as "Beast"), and an exceptionally rigorous core freshman curriculum, historic changes were afoot in America at that time. Our military participation in Vietnam ceased that spring. More impactful to prospective combat USAF Airmen, the Prisoners of War (POWs), were repatriated. Many of these POWs shared accounts about how they got shot down, how they were captured, and how they were mistreated. Their first-person accounts were testimony to how they survived the toxic crucible of starvation and torture. Almost to a man, they cited their reliance on Faith, Family and love of America. These lessons only reinforced the conclusions Tony had embraced.

It is hard to overstate the effect the Vietnam experience had on us. Our academic instructors were almost entirely military officers, most with combat experience. Upon graduation, we were trained as combat pilots by Vietnam Veterans. Their influence on Tony led—at least in part—to Tony being awarded the Hester Award, as "The Outstanding Cadet Who Best Exemplifies the Highest Ideals of Loyalty, Integrity and Courage Award" for our graduating class, a high honor, indeed. The Combat Veterans honed our skills and set our resolve.

**"Man's Flight through Life..."**

Upon graduation, Tony was assigned an Undergraduate Pilot Training slot, in fulfillment of a life-long dream. It is a yearlong course, flying the T-37, the supersonic T-38, plus a painstaking dose of academics, learning flight basics, aircraft systems and military and FAA flight rules. Following pilot training, Tony mastered several combat aircraft (B-52D, OV-10A, A-37B, FB-111). I would suggest, at this point, that learning a new combat aircraft is tantamount to earning a master's degree. One has to know the aircraft's systems (engines, hydraulics, pressurization system, fuel system, oxygen system, ejection seats, appropriate airspeeds associated with different phases of flight, handling characteristics, emergency procedures and all the numbers associated with these items). Too, the weapons systems (radar, bombs/missiles compatible with the aircraft), must be learned. The other part of this is understanding our tactics (different from airframe to airframe, and tactical or strategic mission), the perceived or real threats, (bad guys), tactics and weapons systems that can get a combat aviator shot down or killed.

Tony flourished in this environment. To illustrate, he was the 8th Air Force's nominee for the Jabara Award, awarded to the United States Air Force Academy graduate whose airmanship contributions are of great significance and set them apart from their contemporaries. Striving constantly to excel, he was selected for and graduated from the USAF's Test Pilot School. During this time, he flew dozens of types of aircraft. He ended his USAF flying career as a B-2 Stealth Bomber Squadron Commander, an exceptionally prestigious position.

**"Man's Flight Through Life…"**

Tony proceeded with other forms of continuing education. He completed Squadron Officers School (for junior officers), and Air Command and Staff College (for mid-level officers). He also garnered two Master's degrees, a Master of Science in Systems Management from the University of Southern California, and a Master of Airpower Art and Science from the Air University. He is also a graduate of the Defense Systems Management College.

Tony accomplished all this while nurturing a sound marriage and raising four accomplished children. Two of their children are Service Academy graduates, one from the United States Naval Academy and one from the United States Military Academy. All of them have sound academic accomplishments and are fine patriots. So, not only were Tony and Donna displaying great examples for their children, they endowed them with the motivation to serve their Country and strive for their own accomplishments. Donna and Tony continue, hand in hand, to be the solid foundation of this wonderful family, now blessedly including grandchildren.

Looking past his military and commercial flying careers, Tony has been deeply involved in many faith-based and civic volunteer efforts. Among other things, he has been a Scoutmaster, a volunteer high school track coach and has taught Bible classes and Sunday School. He has served as a Deacon in one congregation and served as an Elder in another. He has tutored high school algebra and has been a Business Mentor at the University of Nevada Innovative Center. More recently, he was the "Air Boss" (Director of Flight Operations) for the National Championship Air Races in Reno. There is a longer list, but Tony will elaborate in his book.

**"Man's Flight Through Life…"**

This leads us to Tony's newest effort, politics. For a first timer, Tony's campaign notably won thirteen of Nevada's seventeen counties for Lieutenant Governor. He placed a close second, a terrific finish given his opponent's name recognition in Nevada's largest populated county, Clark (Las Vegas). His accumulated knowledge and experience have led him, through Faith, Family and love of America, to see and understand that we are on a dangerous and evil path. I concur with him, and hope he runs for the US Senate seat up for election in 2024. I am proud to call Tony a friend and mentor. I assure you he will stick true to his beliefs and will do what he promises. His character: Faith, Family, Patriotism **"…is Sustained by the Power of His Knowledge."**

Colonel John D. Reed, USAF ret.

Colonel Reed is a second-generation United States Air Force Officer and fighter pilot. He graduated from the USAF Academy, Class of '77, with a Bachelor of Science in Management. He has flown several fighter aircraft and won the "Top Gun" award at William Tell '86, the USAF's World-Wide Air-to-Air Weapons Meet. He also served as an F-15C Mission Commander in Operation Desert Storm. He is a graduate of the Defense Language Institute (French) and has a Master of Public Administration from Troy State University, and Master of Science in National Security Strategy from the National War College. He is married to the former Vonice Mary Harr, of Sioux Falls, SD, and they have two children, Matthew and Emily, and grandson, Luke.

# INTRODUCTION

Today many who make their living in the field of academics consider it their job to bash the United States of America. These self-appointed experts like to continually judge the actions of people in the past by endlessly complaining of the bad values that they think the United States was based on, finding almost nothing that is good or worth celebrating. This point of view has serious problems because it is filled with errors, yet it is being forced on children in the classroom.

Parents are becoming more aware of this negative approach in education, especially as the teaching of the basics: reading, writing, and arithmetic, are not of the highest importance anymore. Pushing these subjects to the sidelines is clearly showing up year after year with a steady decline in test scores in these basics for kindergarten through twelfth grade students all over the United States.

It is interesting that those who write much about the terrible problems that were a key part of the founding of our country have greatly benefited from living here, and especially having the opportunity of learning through the education system to reach the level of achievement necessary to publish and to benefit financially from their writing. They claim that the United States is a very bad country from when it was started through today. It is interesting that though they claim the United States is a terrible place, somehow living in it enabled them to become "great" thinkers who know how to direct what needs to happen to correct the terrible problems that cause our country to be such a bad place.

Well, I see those complainers differently. Many who are critical of the United States have not done anything outside the area of academics that might be considered an accomplishment. They have not worked in a business concern nor produced anything of value that would be considered practical, nor worked for someone or some organization that has. It's notable that not many of them have served in the military. Also, it seems that most have not lived for a significant amount of time in another country. I contend they have led such narrow lives that they lack the kind of personal experience necessary to support their viewpoints as well as a world understanding deep enough to accurately identify or evaluate the myriad of problems they continually cite against the United States.

I also see our country differently. As a proud American who had the unique opportunity to travel through Europe frequently and to live on the continents of Africa and Asia in addition to North America while growing up, serving in the United States Air Force, and then later flying for FedEx, I readily challenge those who speak against the United States.

I had the wonderful opportunity to become a pilot in the United States Air Force. The high point of my military career was serving as a test pilot and commanding the 420th Test Squadron at Edwards Air Force Base, California. This squadron tested the B-2, Stealth Bomber, the most expensive combat aircraft ever built and a product of one of the most successful and safest test programs ever conducted. Following my twenty-year Air Force career, I had the unique opportunity to fly internationally for twenty more years for FedEx.

After forty years in the air, I am truly a *Stranger to the Ground*, the title of aviation author Richard Bach's other famous book[2]. Bach skillfully wrote for others to read what those who are blessed to fly actually experience.

So how did a Black American, born in Norfolk, Virginia, to parents who grew up poor have the opportunity to realize his dream of becoming a pilot? I firmly believe my life story shows that all became possible for me because I am a citizen of the United States of America, the greatest country in the world. I was able to work toward my dream unlike many who have lived and are living on this earth who are citizens of another country.

I believe that because of basic American values, I had that opportunity. America needs to hold on to those values, and it is my hope that what I have shared in this memoir will inspire others to do what they can to preserve the American Dream.

> Note: Some stories are referenced several times to establish a timeframe for my life experiences. Also, Chapters 8, 9, and 10 cover my political positions for the reader who might want to know this information directly.

# 1
# FOUNDATION

*"Those who cannot remember the past are condemned to repeat it."*
—**George Santayana,** *American Philosopher*

Both of my parents hailed from North Carolina. They were Black, poor, and grew up in the segregated Jim Crow South governed by Democrat Party-affiliated public office holders. To understand their origins and how those origins and their life journeys helped shape my appreciation for America, it is necessary to look at the political, economic, and physical environment where they lived. Since the geographic areas of the United States are very different from each other, a person's location can be a major contributor to the growth and development of the history he experiences. So, before I introduce you to those particular family members whose values and principles were embedded in my developing sense of what matters as I grew up, I offer the following as a snapshot of the tumult and aftermath that shaped the South my parents knew.

## Historical/Political Background of the South

The American Civil War was the first modern war. During this conflict many of the tactics and operations that make up warfare today were first used and later were seen in the major wars that followed. One key characteristic of the Civil War was "Total War." General William Tecumseh Sherman of the Union Army used this method of fighting (in which battles no longer took place in isolated areas like fields outside of cities leaving the civilian population untouched, but took place anywhere, including cities and thus involving civilian casualties) in his 'March to the Sea' where he destroyed everything in his path. This is also called the "scorched earth" policy. This left the eleven States who separated or seceded from the Union, called the Confederacy, economically, politically, and morally defeated. Reconstruction (1865-1877) was a plan developed by the U.S. government immediately following the Civil War to rebuild the Southern States that seceded. Reconstruction was carried out by allowing the Confederate States to come back into the Union and building a society where the newly freed slaves could live freely in a place where many people in the local area were very unfriendly toward them.[3] The three phases of Reconstruction were: presidential, congressional, final.[4] In the first phase of presidential Reconstruction (1865-1867), the two primary goals were to bring the Southern States back into the Union as quickly as possible and to give the newly freed slaves freedom by removing laws that kept them from being hired or from owning property.[5]

The second phase was congressional Reconstruction. In this phase, the plan was to bring about full political equality for the former slaves, to help them economically by giving out forty-acres-and-a-mule, and to punish the former Confederates.[6] During this period Blacks joined the political process through the Republican Party and were elected to various political offices on the local, state, and national levels.

The final phase was greatly affected by the Hayes-Tilden Compromise of 1877,[7] when public support for the initial goals of Reconstruction decreased significantly. The Compromise allowed white supremacy to return through state governments again having "home rule," which was able to happen when the Federal Troops were withdrawn from the South. These events permitted the return of subjugation of Black Americans by the Democrats, who brought back the Black Codes,[8] racial segregation, and the Jim Crow laws.[9] So, the former slaves were once again harassed and forced out of political office.[10] They were returned to a life where no opportunity to seek self-improvement was forced upon them.[11] During this period the small, but greatly appreciated, political gains achieved by Blacks completely disappeared. Discrimination against Blacks became the normal way of life for the southern states, especially for North Carolina twelve years after the Civil War, and for many years to come.

---

## GRADY FAMILY HISTORY BEGINS[12]

In the 1870s North Carolina was governed by Democrat Party office holders. Southern Pines, an important area on my family tree, lies within Moore County in North Carolina. The city is characterized by sandy ground and forests of pine trees. Southern Pines was made up of two communities when it began in the 19th century. Immigrants from Scotland and temporary visitors from the Northern United States who wanted to spend time away from the cold winters were the main groups that lived in East Southern Pines.[13] The Blacks lived in West Southern Pines, which is one of the first African-American towns to be incorporated in North Carolina.[14]

### Russell Lee Grady

My grandfather, Russell Lee Grady, was born in Lillington, North Carolina on August 8, 1871. His parents were Evander and Mary Grady. Russell had two siblings, Tarlton Evander and Mary. Eventually, the family migrated to Midway, North Carolina, located between Southern Pines and Aberdeen.

The source of his academic training is a mystery since he was born six years following the end of slavery. That said, he was a good reader, a competent writer, and he was proficient in arithmetic. Throughout his life there were many times he proved that he was capable of doing these activities very well.

Russell later lived in Southern Pines where he ran a restaurant, and that is where he met my grandmother, Alice Viola Harris (called Viola). The restaurant was a town favorite, and many remarked that Russell was a sharp dresser. Although Russell and Viola were excellent cooks, they left the restaurant business because men making passes at Viola, and often violating her personal space, made things too uncomfortable for her at work.

Russell and Viola married and had eight children: Russell Lee Grady Jr., Augustine Herman Grady, Gordon Edward Grady, Walter Anthony Grady, Nettie Catherine Grady, Oliver Eugene Grady, John Evander Grady, and Roberta Viola Grady. My grandparents were both Christians by their faith in the Lord Jesus Christ. Russell was a Methodist and Viola was a Baptist. The children received most of their religious training in the Baptist Church.

Though Russell did not attend church regularly, at breakfast every Sunday morning, he would read the Bible and lead the family in prayer. Sometimes, instead of reading the Scripture, he would ask his children to recite a Bible verse from memory. An amusing family story recounts how he would not allow any of the children to complete this task by merely saying, "Jesus Wept," from John 11:35, which is the shortest verse in the Bible. Russell did not have the family sing hymns because he did not like to sing, nor was he drawn to make music. He did not play an instrument. However, he did like listening to classical music and gave his full support to his son Gordon's musical training. Russell made sure that his children were well behaved.

To support the family, Russell labored in many different jobs. Southern Pines was a resort for many of the wealthy during the winter, especially for those who enjoyed playing golf. One of Russell's jobs was being a caddie. Many working families in the town derived some, if not all, of their income from caddying. He also served as a caretaker, ensuring that his clients' homes were heated by servicing and monitoring their furnaces. This line of work caused him to rise early in the morning to make his rounds, firing up the furnaces and banking[15] them to keep the homes warm throughout the day. He repeated this routine in the evening.

In the summer Russell did landscaping for many of the wealthy Southern Pines natives as well as for some of the vacationing winter residents. There was also a time where he worked as a foreman for some of the blackberry and peach farmers. He was responsible for finding and hiring workers, supervising their transportation to the farm, and deciding where they worked.

Because Russell was very good at arithmetic, he was a great help to his children as they studied the subject. He especially liked doing fractions. However, when his children got to algebra, they were on their own, for that area of mathematics was not familiar to him. Russell was an avid reader as well. He enjoyed poring over newspapers and magazines and regularly read about current events and politics, especially what was happening in the federal government.

Every Sunday he visited with one of the few neighbors who owned a radio so he could listen to President Roosevelt's "Fireside Chats."[16] During this time in the United States, people were very concerned when Social Security legislation was introduced. Many political discussions took place throughout the community to figure out what would happen after the government put this plan in place. Russell was swamped with people asking him questions because they knew he read quite a bit and knew much about politics.

West Southern Pines was the segregated area of the city, and at that time, the only city in North Carolina governed by Blacks.[17] The city elected a mayor and a board of commissioners. Russell served as a commissioner and was next in line to become mayor. However, West Southern Pines was incorporated and combined with the White area of the city before the election, so Russell never became the mayor.[18]

During the last six years of his life, Russell suffered from severe asthmatic attacks, which prevented him from continuing to work. He died from a heart attack caused by the medicine he took for an asthma attack on July 3, 1937. When Russell died his son Gordon was twenty years old and working in Greensboro, North Carolina, while preparing for his second year of college. Russell's passing was a hardship for the whole family and particularly for Grandmother Grady. When Russell died, she took all the children to live with her mother during the summer.

## Alice Viola Grady

My grandmother was born Alice Viola Harris in 1892 and passed away in 1974. After my grandfather died, she served as a cook for the Boyd family. James and Katharine Boyd were a famous wealthy family who lived in Southern Pines.[19] James was a writer, and their family roots began in Pennsylvania.[20] The family wealth came from the railroad business.[21] Viola was very resourceful. She continued to raise her family on the salary of a domestic employee. Though the Grady family was poor, the family thrived.

My cousin Alice remembers that Viola could make very delicious meals that filled a person up out of the scraps or unpopular cuts of meat she was able to get. Alice recounts how she didn't understand until she was older that, when Viola started with flour, added a few ingredients including cinnamon, and baked it into rolls, she was watching was Viola effortlessly making perfect handmade cinnamon rolls.

Viola encouraged her children to take their education very seriously. She would say, "knowledge is power." Though the education system in North Carolina was segregated, she encouraged her children to attend college, a choice that was made possible through a business arrangement she made with the Boyd family. Instead of paying into her Social Security, they offered to pay her children's college tuition. Within the family the children agreed to take care of Viola after her working years, if Viola agreed to this opportunity.

The children followed through with their part of this agreement. My Uncle Gordon, her third born, moved to Philadelphia and eventually had Grandmother Grady come live in that city. A few years later other members of the family, including my immediate family, also moved there and helped with her care. Three of her eight children took advantage of the opportunity that the Boyds offered to attend college. My Uncle Gordon attended North Carolina A&T, my father, Walter, attended Hampton Institute, and my Aunt Nettie was admitted to Johnson C. Smith.

These were some of the first Historically Black Colleges, created for the purpose of educating Blacks who had been denied education due to Jim Crow. The overall goal of these colleges was to graduate well-educated people who could become teachers to educate younger Blacks at all levels in the school system.[22]

In her later years, Viola was stricken with arthritis. My earliest memories are of her in a wheelchair. Though this limited her freedom of movement, she was always very independent. She used the "L" end of a curtain rod to help her move things she needed that were just out of her reach. To reach items on the table, she used a short rod and a longer one for items up on a shelf.

Very creative with her hands, she knitted and crocheted. Some of her work included beautiful comforters, scarves, and doilies with woven shapes of animals on them. I remember sachets containing pine needles that gave off a pleasing aroma. She even taught me how to crochet when I was about six years old. Wintertime was my favorite time for visiting with her because, during that season, she roasted chestnuts. The aroma was captivating, and they tasted delicious.

Viola was a devout Christian. Her Bible stood out in the small apartment where she lived. She would earn money making handkerchiefs for the Deacons of her church. They were quite colorful, and she made them from odd cuts of cloth. Being confined to a wheelchair prevented her from leaving her apartment when she might want to. On Sundays she would listen to sermons on the radio where the Black preachers could be heard.

I remember visiting her shortly after Apollo astronauts Neil Armstrong and Buzz Aldrin landed on the moon on July 20, 1969. Since I was very interested in the space program, I was excited to discuss with her this monumental event. After listening to me she remarked, "Tony, they didn't land on the moon. The moon is in a socket, and you can't land on it." I immediately looked at my mother who gave me a smile and a wink, at which point I realized that I shouldn't try to continue that conversation. Grandmother Grady was a character!

I have fond memories of her and remember the solemn day that she died. I was allowed emergency leave from the United States Air Force Academy during my freshman year to attend her funeral, which was a very memorable event. It was the first such event I had attended for a family member. Processing that I would never see her again took a while after I viewed her lifeless body in the casket. She was buried back in Southern Pines, North Carolina, in Woodlawn Cemetery next to Grandfather Grady.

## Gordon Edward Grady

My Uncle, Gordon Edward Grady, born on September 11, 1917, was the third child of Viola and Russell Grady. At a young age he showed a strong aptitude for manipulating numbers, which eventually helped him to become a bookkeeper in a local store in Southern Pines. I once asked him why he excelled in mathematics, and he responded that while working in the store he would always determine the change from financial transactions in his head. This practice was in addition to the tutoring his father provided in helping my uncle with his schoolwork.

Gordon graduated from West Southern Pines Colored High School in 1934. He then attended North Carolina Agricultural and Technical College, now known as North Carolina A&T State University. There, he earned a Bachelor of Science Degree in Electrical Engineering and was certified to teach high school mathematics and physics. This achievement was tremendous for a Black American during this time.

Gordon arrived at A&T with the desire to work hard and do well but did not have the money or means to pay his tuition. He shared with Cousin Alice that he, "went to college with a shirt and a small shopping bag full of ties." Fortunately, the Boyds helped him in this area by paying the tuition for him.

Gordon also received a scholarship that required him to work in the kitchen throughout his college career. Today this would be considered a "work study" program. He worked at other jobs to support himself during those college years as well.

Getting ahead wasn't easy. Like his father, Gordon was troubled with asthma. Though he earned a degree in electrical engineering, racial divisions in the United States prevented him from being employed in that field. So, when he returned home in 1940, he taught math, physics, and chemistry at his high school, West Southern Pines Colored High School. Gordon also worked as a contractor.

During World War II, Uncle Gordon worked as an electrician at the Naval Yard in Norfolk, Virginia. His chronic asthma eventually caused him to move to Philadelphia, Pennsylvania, where he worked for several companies providing technical and engineering services. However, he was still not officially employed as an engineer.

While in Philadelphia, he continued to better himself by qualifying to enter the Moore School of Electrical Engineering at the University of Pennsylvania. This school had a great reputation and was highly thought of. Uncle Gordon graduated in 1958 with a master's degree in electrical engineering, another high and rare achievement for a Black American during this era. After graduation he taught evening classes in radio servicing and electrical wiring to veterans.

In his book, *A Struggle Worthy of Note: The Engineering and Technological Education of Black Americans*, author David E. Wharton recalls the following conversation with Gordon:

> "In 1951, in response to a classified ad announcing openings for engineers, Grady applied for an opening at the Honeywell plant in Philadelphia. In his telephone conversation with the personnel manager, he assumed the job would be his since his experience dovetailed with the job requirements. However, when he arrived for the interview, there were other job applicants seated in the waiting room. Soon the personnel manager came out to page Mr. Gordon Grady, an engineering applicant. As he eyed the room full of men, it became increasingly obvious that the applicant he sought was the lone Black man in the group. In the interview that followed, Grady was told that a young man had come in 'just a moment ago' with qualifications that exceeded his and **that** young man—...not Grady—would be given the job.
>
> "The personnel office was glass-fronted, allowing a person passing in the hall to look into the office. As Grady left this appointment, he looked back with disgust at the personnel manager; as he did so, he saw his resume thrown into the trash can."[23]

Wharton writes later in the book that at one point a manager gave my uncle an opportunity to work as an engineer. However, soon afterwards he was denied the position due to the other employed engineers threatening to walk out if the company hired a Black man. This unfortunate situation clearly shows my uncle's strength of character to overcome the frustrations, hurts, and pains caused by humiliation and the unfair treatment that Black college-trained professionals had to silently endure during this point in history. In the face of the racial tensions of his era, he continued to push himself to move forward.

It took fourteen years before my Uncle Gordon was finally recognized as an engineer. In 1954 Gordon was hired as an engineer at the Naval Air Material Center (NAMC) located in the Philadelphia Navy Yard complex. His work focused on missile projects involving aircraft instrumentation, electronic science, and research engineering.

Though Gordon was finally recognized as a full-fledged engineer at this time, he had little hope to advance. As a result, Gordon decided to leave the Naval Air Material Center when the late President John F. Kennedy announced his goal of putting a man on the moon by the end of the decade.

Following the President's announcement, General Electric (G.E.) looked for engineers to work in the field of space science. In February of 1962 Gordon was hired by G.E. as a systems test engineer to work in the unmanned spacecraft section of the Space Environmental Test Facility. This facility was in King of Prussia, Pennsylvania. G.E. placed Gordon on a team of engineers and technicians focused on testing the strength of the structure and how well a spacecraft flew when exposed to the harsh and extreme conditions of outer space. The team's work also included testing the equipment and other material that would be used in space and during the first walk on the moon. Gordon was responsible for simulating the heat that the spacecraft would experience from the sun.

At last, Uncle Gordon was given the opportunity to fully use his engineering training! He also taught engineering subjects for Penn State University in the school's Continuing Education Department. Once the goal of a man walking on the moon was reached, G.E. ended the research phase that made the moon landing possible and moved Gordon to the company facility located in Lynn, Massachusetts.

In this new location, he was responsible for updating test cell equipment and served as an Instrumentation Engineer. Gordon became a manager of the Advanced Instrumentation Unit in 1972 and remained in this position until 1983 when he retired. Professionally, Gordon held two offices in the Institute of Environmental Sciences. The technical papers he wrote led to Uncle Gordon being awarded a *Fellow* membership. When he retired, he was made an *Honorary Fellow* with a lifetime membership in the Institute.

Gordon also actively participated in his community. His faith in God was central to his life. He was a member of Grace Episcopal Church for more than forty years serving in several offices including Vestryman, Junior Warden, Senior Warden, Lector, and Chalice. Gordon Grady passed away on May 10, 2021. It was my honor to speak at his funeral, and I find Wharton's words about my uncle very apt:

> "Gordon Grady is important because he typifies many African Americans who overcame the denials of a segregated society. His story is the story of an individual assuming an ever-expanding role throughout his professional career."[24]

Uncle Gordon's daughter, Paula, rightly characterized his life as one where he used wisdom, perseverance, and faith to overcome those denials.

## Walter Anthony Grady, Sr.

My father, Walter Anthony Grady, was born on July 29, 1920. He was the fourth child born to Russell and Viola Grady. My father did not share with me much about his childhood. I was made aware of his family's meager means when he recounted that during the wintertime they would gather around the coal burning stove in the kitchen to warm up. Then they would run and jump in bed and get under the covers and try to get to sleep before the warmth left them and the cold would eventually set in. He also mentioned watching the wealthy residents of Southern Pines play golf. He always liked to watch the game.

My father graduated from West Southern Pines High School on May 25, 1939. With the help of the Boyd family, he was able to attend Hampton Institute, now Hampton University in Norfolk, Virginia. Hampton Institute is one of the original Historically Black Colleges and Universities (HBCUs) with an interesting history that exemplifies the American success story.[25]

## THE HAMPTON INSTITUTE HISTORY

In 1861, early in the American Civil War, the Union Army controlled Fort Monroe, which was located at the mouth of the Chesapeake in Hampton, Virginia. Historians note that "Union General Benjamin Butler decreed that any escaping slaves reaching Union lines would be considered 'contraband of war' and would not be returned to bondage."

This opportunity caused a flood of Blacks to enter the fort. A camp built outside of Fort Monroe to house these newly freed slaves was called "The Grand Contraband Camp" and was the first fully operating African American Community.[26] Since the South was controlled by public officials from the Democrat Party, they forbade the education of any Blacks. This edict was one of many used to suppress the Blacks in the South.

To help solve this problem for this new community, Mary Peake, who was a Free Negro, taught the first class in the community which had about twenty students and met under an oak tree.[27] Later this oak tree is where President Lincoln's Emancipation Proclamation was read, and that tree has been known as the Emancipation Oak from that moment on.[28] General Butler obtained government funds to continue the work that Mary Peake started, and founded the Butler School for Negro children that taught them reading, writing, arithmetic, geography, grammar, and housekeeping.[29]

Union Brigadier General Samuel C. Armstrong was assigned as Superintendent of the Freedmen's Bureau of the Ninth District of Virginia in 1866.[30] The bureau was tasked with working on issues related to newly freed Blacks living in the South. Armstrong, who served as a missionary in Hawaii before the Civil War, used his experience working with the mission school there to start the Hampton Normal and Agricultural Institute on April 1, 1868.[31] It was right next to the Butler School and had the following purpose:

> "...[T]o train selected negro youth who should go out and teach and lead their people first by example, by getting land and homes; to give them not a dollar that they could earn for themselves; to teach respect for labor, to replace stupid drudgery with skilled hands, and in this way to build up an industrial system for the sake not only of self-support and intelligent labor, but also for the sake of character."[32]

The Butler School became the Whittier School in 1889 and was used to teach the students of Hampton Normal School.[33] Perhaps the most famous graduate of Hampton Institute was Booker T. Washington, who later in 1881 helped to start Tuskegee Institute in Alabama.[34]

---

Following the educational plan for Hampton students, Dad first studied a vocation, also called a trade. He was certified on June 2, 1942, as a cabinet-maker tradesman. Before entering Hampton, Dad had worked part time as a bricklayer. After a while he'd realized that he did not like that type of really hard manual labor. He wanted to do something less physically demanding, such as cabinet making.

As a young child I remember that the twin beds my sister and I slept on during our younger years while living in Philadelphia were made by my father. Now after raising four children of my own and moving several times during my professional life, especially while in the military, I remember how useful the beds he made for us were. They each had two large drawers on the side that could store extra pillows and linens or anything else that would fit. The beds were mounted on wheels that could be locked by hand, making them easy to move. In short, they were quite efficient. Dad also made the coffee table that was in front of the couch in our living room. He was an expert craftsman.

Continuing his education at Hampton, two years later, Dad earned his Bachelor of Science degree in Vocational Education on January 31, 1944. He remained at Hampton Institute for four years and served as an instructor until my mother graduated from the same school in 1948. The next year he earned a Master of Arts in Education from New York University. He went on to hold teaching posts at Cheyney State College in Philadelphia, Pennsylvania, Texas Southern University in Houston, Texas, and Virginia State College in Norfolk, Virginia.

Notably, Dad went on to hold a number of positions in foreign service, beginning with a special United States Agency for International Development (USAID) project in vocational education in Indonesia from 1957-1959. From 1963-1967 he served on the staff of the International Labor Organization (ILO) of the United Nations in Lagos, Nigeria. After acting as educational advisor and then deputy director of education in Canto, Vietnam, Dad received the Award for Civilian Service in 1968. He was recognized for his work in provincial development assistance in 1979 by the Republic of the Philippines. He also received an award for distinguished service by the USAID when he retired in 1985.

Like his brother Gordon, Dad had a remarkable journey of upward accomplishments. He passed away on January 13, 1996 at his home in the Poconos in Albrightsville, Pennsylvania.

## Dorothy Elizabeth Hunter

My Mother, Dorothy Elizabeth Hunter, was born on the last day of February in 1922, in Mooresville, North Carolina, a town that started slowly. In the late 1800s families who farmed moved there from towns like Charlotte and Salisbury that were nearby.[35] In 1873, the North Carolina General Assembly allowed the town to change its name from the Village of Moore to the Town of Mooresville since a group of men including John F. Moore asked for a charter."[36] The railroad was very important to the growth of the town:

> "...it transported the large amount of cotton produced in Iredell County in the 1800s. An economic boom in the 1890s led to the

Mooresville Cotton Mills, Lorne Cotton Seed Mill, Big Oak Rolling Mill, and the Mooresville Creamery. By the start of the 20th century, Mooresville was home to several more textile, sawmills, cotton gins, lumber yards, and a foundry."[37]

Mom never knew who her parents were. She was raised by her grandmother until age fourteen when her grandmother died. After the death of her grandmother, she went to live with some cousins who also lived in Mooresville. She received letters from her mother until she was thirteen years old. Then they stopped.

Though she grew up at the lower end of the economic spectrum, Mom always sought to better herself. She never dwelled on where she was, but set her focus on moving where she wanted to be. Mom had dreams.

An encounter Mom shared with her cousins was that one day while finishing up her cleaning duties in a hospital where she worked part time as a teenager, she saw some of the other girls with whom she attended school. Mom had to work in order to buy school clothes. At that moment, realizing that these girls did not need to work for their school clothing so they were freer to do the things that interested them, Mom decided she wanted more out of life.

The cousins then began helping Mom to look for other job opportunities. They discovered ads in the newspaper for domestic workers to come and work in the homes of wealthy people in New Jersey. After some discussion, Mom and her cousins decided that this would give her more options in life, which meant that at the age of sixteen, Mom moved to New Jersey to answer the agency ad.

The first job she took did not turn out well. One example she cited concerned the time a carnival came to town. She wanted to go and see it. She had never seen a carnival before. When she asked her employer about going, she was told to mow the lawn first, and once she'd finished, she could go. She had never mowed the lawn before, and it was rather large. As she worked the time passed, and the carnival closed before she finished mowing.

Since this was a task that she had never done before, she felt like her employer intentionally asked her to do this to prevent her from attending the carnival. During this time, it was not uncommon for domestic workers to be exploited, to be regularly asked to do such things as work on their days off, for example.

Eventually she was hired by another family in New Jersey, that of Mr. and Mrs. Mountcastle.[38] After a period, the Mountcastles realized that Mom always worked hard and showed much initiative. They also realized that she wanted to improve herself by seeking more education. After some discussion Mrs. Mountcastle told my mother that she could continue to live with them, but instead of her normal workload, she would attend another year of high school. Her schooling in North Carolina was not advanced enough to prepare her to attend college.

While Mom was finishing up high school, Mrs. Mountcastle also saw to it that she was exposed to more activities that gave her an increased cultural awareness. As an example, the Mountcastles bought her tickets to attend shows on Broadway in New York City.

My mother spoke of one time when she attended a show where Paul Robeson performed. Mr. Robeson was a Black concert singer who became famous internationally between the First and Second World Wars. In addition, he was an All-American Football star who played for Rutgers.[39] This was a rare and tremendous opportunity for a Black young woman who grew up poor in North Carolina.

The Jim Crow South controlled by Democratic Party public office holders did not view that it was proper to give such opportunities to those who were Black. After high school my mother was accepted into the nursing program at Hampton Institute. The Mountcastles paid for her college tuition and bought her ticket to travel there.

When it came time for Mom to leave New Jersey, Mr. Mountcastle explained in detail how she would travel to Norfolk, Virginia by train and then steamboat. When I think about my mother's journey at this stage in her life, I realize how difficult it must have been and how nervous she probably was doing many things that were so unfamiliar to her. Today, no one really thinks about traveling long distances; however, in 1936 this must have been hard for her.

Each step along the way that led to her traveling from Mooresville, North Carolina, to attend college in Hampton, Virginia, clearly shows Mom's strength of character. I can't imagine the fortitude and determination Mom must have had at sixteen that made her willing to work for others in another state and at the same time able to keep her focus on eventually entering college. She overcame her fears, worked hard, and saw her dreams turned into reality with the generous and gracious help of the Mountcastles.

Mom met Dad at Hampton and graduated from the institution with a nursing degree. They were married in the Bronx, New York, on February 29, 1948.

## Mom and Dad Build a Family—Have Suitcase, Will Travel

In 1950 my parents relocated to Houston, where Dad worked as a vocational education instructor at Texas Southern University. On October 13, 1951, my sister, Walteen Penelope Grady was born. The family returned to Virginia when, in 1954, Dad took a teaching job at Norfolk State College.

On December 5, 1955, I was born and named Walter Anthony Grady Jr. Since Dad and I had the same first name, I was nicknamed Tony. I was told that I was also named after the doctor who delivered me, Dr. Tony. He worked with my mother since she worked as a nurse in Norfolk.

Early on, Mom made it clear to my father that she did not want the children to receive their education in the segregated schools of the South. A job offer made fulfilling her wish. The country of Indonesia asked the United States to help them with converting some of their cottage industries into businesses. This request went to Tuskegee Institute, now Tuskegee University, a Historically Black College located in Tuskegee, Alabama.[40]

A selection board was formed at Tuskegee to review people who might be able to carry out this task. Dad was one of the people that the committee interviewed, and he was eventually selected for the job. Our family moved from Norfolk, Virginia to Philadelphia, Pennsylvania and joined my Uncle Gordon. We lived on different floors of the same house and we helped more with the care of Grandmother Grady.

In 1958, Dad was sent by Tuskegee Institute on a one-year grant to Jakarta, the capitol of Indonesia, located on the island of Java. Our family was to join him as soon as he was able to find a place for us to live. But after he'd found a house for us, the instability in the government led to clashes in the city. This situation prevented the family from going to Indonesia, and Dad finished his grant work with us far away.

While in Indonesia Dad was told that, though he was only on a one-year grant, the United Nations (U.N.) had a permanent office that managed the type of work he was doing in many areas of the world. Someone suggested that he apply to this office for a permanent job. Dad returned to Philadelphia and applied to the International Labor Organization (ILO), which is an agency inside the U.N. that was created in 1919 in the Treaty of Versailles.[41]

The draft committee regarding the constitution of the organization was chaired by Samuel Gompers of the American Federation of Labor.[42] The constitution stated that the purpose of the organization was to ensure that the member countries created the necessary working conditions for all, especially children, women, and older people; it listed "recognition of the principle of freedom of association, the organization of vocational and technical education and other measures..."[43] as its goals.

My father was hired by the ILO to work in the vocational and technical education area. The ILO sent my father to work in Lagos, Nigeria, in 1963. Our family traveled there together. We lived on the outside of Lagos in an area known as Yaba. The apartment we lived in was on the campus of the Yaba College of Technology.

Dad worked there for three years. During this time my father met people who were employed by the United States doing the same kind of work he was doing. Their organization was the United States Agency for International Development (USAID). Some members of the agency suggested that Dad think about working for them. He did, and when it was time to leave Nigeria and return home to Philadelphia, Dad resigned from the ILO and applied to work for USAID.

USAID was created in 1961 when President Kennedy signed the Foreign Assistance Act which gathers three groups into one: the Mutual Security Agency, the Foreign Operations Administration, and the International Cooperation Administration.[44] Explaining the need for USAID, America's 35th President observed:

"There is no escaping our obligations: our moral obligations as a wise leader and good neighbor in the interdependent community of free nations – our economic obligations as the wealthiest people in a world of largely poor people, as a nation no longer dependent upon the loans from abroad that once helped us develop our own economy – and our political obligations as the single largest counter to the adversaries of freedom."[45]

USAID is the nonpolitical side of the U.S. State Department through which money was given to help lesser developed countries around the world. Though a much more complex organization today, originally USAID was made up of five major divisions: agriculture, education, medical, public safety, and the United States Information Service (USIS) that is now called The United States Information Agency. In 1967 Dad was hired by USAID in the education division and sent to Bien Hoa, the Republic of South Vietnam. Dad's major work involved helping the South Vietnamese government build and staff technical and vocational schools.

Since the Vietnam War was going on, the family was sent to Bangkok, Thailand as a "safe haven," as it was referred to by the U.S. government at that time. I remained in Bangkok, Thailand from the age of twelve until I graduated high school from the International School of Bangkok in 1973. From there I was selected and attended the United States Air Force Academy.

American Values at Work: Though they were Black and grew up poor in the Jim Crow South governed by Democrat Party public office holders who did not demonstrate much regard for the welfare of Black southerners, my parents, my Grady grandparents, and other family members, helped along by generous benefactors, became successful. Working hard, achieving academic competence, and believing in a better future—all values at America's heart—were guideposts for my family from its beginnings. It was those same values that launched me into the sometimes unwelcoming world and made it possible for me to forge my path. My story comes next to illustrate why I believe it is vital for our country to uphold and continue those values.

# AMERICAN VALUES: ANOTHER VOICE

My father Walter A. Grady Sr, and his mother, Alice Viola Grady on January 19, 1944, when he graduated with a Bachelor of Science from Hampton Institute located in Norfolk Virginia.

Walter A. Grady Sr, and Dorothy H. Grady, my Mother and Father in our house on Uber St. In Philadelphia, Fall of 1986.

My Uncle, Gordon Edward Grady on his ninetieth birthday in Salem Massachusetts in 2007. His broad smile was characteristic of him.

# 2

# MY FLIGHT PATH: AN OVERVIEW

*"The journey of a thousand miles begins with a single step."*
—**Lao Tzu,** *Chinese Philosopher*

I enjoyed my time at university, and I was busy. The United States Air Force Academy, located in Colorado Springs, Colorado, sits at the base of the Rampart Range, majestic mountains that rise above the academy's silver gray buildings. The setting is picture perfect. Freshmen are affectionately called Doolies (a title derived from a Greek word, doulos, meaning slave). I was a member of Cadet Squadron 29 for my Freshman year, and I was part of Squadron 21 for my last three years. I participated in intercollegiate athletics as a member of the track and field team. I was also a member of the protestant choir and the cadet chorale.

Commissioned as a second lieutenant, I graduated on June 1, 1977, with a Bachelor of Science Degree in Astronautical Engineering. That makes me a rocket scientist! Well, then again, maybe not.... I was selected for undergraduate pilot training and headed off to Williams Air Force Base, in Chandler, Arizona, just outside Phoenix.

Pilot training lasted a year and prepared students to become air force pilots. The first or primary training aircraft we flew was the T-37B. It was very forgiving in that the student pilot could make errors, but the good flight characteristics kept the airplane flying well. Kind of like a dog that allows the baby, who is a new addition to the family, to pull on its ear and tail, but won't bite because the animal understands. This airplane was well suited for all of us learning how to fly a jet aircraft.

The second, or advanced training aircraft, was the T-38A. This airplane could fly faster than the speed of sound, which is 761.2 mph at sea level. We affectionately called it the "White Rocket." Its flight characteristics were more demanding, so there was a much narrower margin for error when flying this airplane. If you didn't pay attention, it would kill you.

After graduating from pilot training in 1978, I was assigned to Carswell Air Force Base, located in Fort Worth, Texas, where I flew the B-52D Heavy Bomber. I was a member of the 9th Bomb Squadron of the 7th Bombardment Wing. These bombers flew in Vietnam and were quite old. It could carry eighty-four five-hundred-pound conventional bombs, the largest bombload that any Air Force Bomber could carry at that time. One outstanding life event of mine that occurred in Fort Worth is that I met and fell for my future wife, Donna, there.

In 1981 I had my first assignment outside of the United States. I left Carswell Air Force Base and reported at Osan Air Base in the Republic of South Korea. I first flew the OV-10A and then the A-37B. I was in the 19th Tactical Air Support Squadron, which was part of the 51st Air Composite Wing. Flying in Korea was very enjoyable. Becoming familiar with the geographic landmarks from the air and knowing exactly where the Demilitarized Zone or DMZ between North and South Korea started and ended was one of the primary responsibilities of my job.

In the middle of the South Korea assignment, realizing that I was halfway around the world from the woman I loved, I returned to the United States and married my sweetheart, Donna, who was still living in Fort Worth. We were married on June 10, 1983, in the United States Air Force Academy Chapel in Colorado. Not only was the setting beautiful but it brought back many of the fond memories of choir and chorale performances from my cadet years. Very soon after the wedding, Donna returned to Korea with me.

After Korea my next assignment began in 1984 at Plattsburgh Air Force Base in upstate New York. The City of Plattsburgh was located next to Lake Champlain and about sixty miles south of Montreal, Canada. The summers were beautiful with dense green trees and bushes as far as you could see. In the fall, the turning of the leaves was breathtaking, showing all the golds, reds, and oranges of fall. The winters, however, were brutal. The snow could completely cover the car in the driveway and temperatures could reach forty degrees below zero. That was cold!

I flew the FB-111A at Plattsburgh in the 529th Bomb Squadron, a unit of the 380th Bomb Wing. The FB-111A was a medium bomber in which the pilot could move or sweep the wings back to make the airplane look almost like an arrowhead, allowing it to slice through the air with ease and accelerate to very high speeds. This airplane could fly faster than the speed of sound.

We also welcomed John Robert Grady, our first child there. In 1988, I was selected to attend the United States Air Force Test Pilot School, located at Edwards Air Force Base in Southern California, so we packed up and went west. Edwards is about eighty-eight miles north of Los Angeles, and it is one of the four military test pilot schools in the world.[46] All four schools put pilots through a rigorous course of study to transform them into Test Pilots capable of testing any new experimental airplane. Non-pilots also attend these schools and are trained to become essential support members of advanced test programs. These schools have exchange programs and accept students from different branches of the military as well as students from different allied countries. The school is about six months long and attempts to expose the pilots to the widest range of aviation during the training course.

After Edwards Air Force Base, later that year, I was assigned to Wright-Patterson Air Force Base in Dayton, Ohio, the birthplace of aviation. Though most people think that the birthplace of aviation was in Kitty-Hawk, North Carolina, they are mistaken. Though the first flight took place in Kitty-Hawk, the Wright Brothers developed and tested their aviation theories in their bicycle shop in Dayton, Ohio, where they lived. Dayton is where aviation was invented. Kitty-Hawk was chosen for the first flight because its early morning calm wind conditions provided the brothers with the best chance for successfully making their firm belief that man could fly become reality.

At Wright-Patterson, I oversaw the test team that helped to choose a new advanced training aircraft for the Air Force called the T-1A Jayhawk. Our next two children were born at the Wright-Patterson Air Force Base hospital, but once again, a mere twenty-two months after arriving in Dayton, we had suitcases to pack and moving arrangements to make. I was sent to Maxwell Air Force Base in Montgomery, Alabama, where the Air University is located.

I first attended Air Command and Staff College; then I was selected to be a member of the second class to attend the School for Advance Airpower Studies, now called the School for Advanced Airpower and Space Studies. The purpose of Air Command and Staff College is to train officers in professional military education. The graduates are prepared to go into various jobs where they might serve as staff officers throughout the Air Force or another branch of the military. The school also has an exchange program with other military services, other countries, and with civilians from the private sector. The School for Advanced Airpower and Space Studies is the Air Force's premier strategy school designed to instill the tenets of airpower in those who might become part of the staff of a combatant commander, or four-star general charged with conducting combat operations in a specific area of the world. Our fourth and last child was born during the time we were in Alabama.

After Maxwell Air Force Base, in 1992 I was assigned to the Pentagon in Washington, D.C., at Air Force Headquarters on the air staff, working for the Director of Combat Forces, leading his long-range-attack team. There I planned and made recommendations on how to organize funding for all the Air Force Bombers. I also gave recommendations to strengthen and improve Air Force strategy. I learned much about how the U.S. President's budget is determined and how the military and other government organizations receive funds from Congress as it goes through the budget process.

Not allowed to get too comfortable in our nation's capital, Donna and I were soon coordinating yet another move. I had been chosen to serve as the operations officer, or second-in-command, of the 420th Flight Test Squadron, the organization responsible for testing and certifying the B-2 Stealth Bomber. This great opportunity for advancement sent me back to Edwards Air Force Base in 1994, where I flew B-2 test and evaluation flights and flew the F-16 as a safety chase pilot to watch and assist during B-2 flight test operations.

Moving the family multiple times while I served in the Air Force was a challenge. Since our children were very young, school was not a complicating factor. As they aged we decided to home school our children to keep their education consistent instead of entering them into multiple schools. In Chapter 7, The Tribe, I will discuss this more in detail.

Each place we lived had its advantages. By the time we lived in Washington, D.C., Donna enjoyed taking the children to many of the museums and monuments in the nation's capital. Also, my children had the opportunity to meet many children from various backgrounds and countries. In Dayton, Ohio, we hosted a foreign exchange student and his children for dinner one evening which everyone participated in with great pleasure and enthusiasm. Overall, experiencing so much of the world and our country benefited the members of our family.

The high point of my Air Force service came in 1996, though, when the Air Force selected me to command the B-2 test squadron. The job was demanding, but also extremely rewarding. I worked with outstanding people both military and civilian who, through teamwork during the final phases of the test program, were able to deliver the B-2 ready for combat to the pilots called war fighters at Whiteman Air Force Base, located near Knob Noster, Missouri.

In 1997, after twenty years, I retired from the Air Force as a Lieutenant Colonel. I had enjoyed a wonderful career.

During the next phase of my life, I flew for FedEx for twenty-years. I first flew out of FedEx's Asian hub located in Subic Bay, Republic of the Philippines, from 1998 to 1999, and I welcomed the chance for my children to experience living outside of the United States. Living overseas would give them first-hand knowledge of how the United States compared to other countries.

While in the Philippines, I flew as a First Officer on the Airbus A-300 to various countries in Southeast Asia. I was able to see how many of the cities I visited twenty years earlier during the time I lived in Bangkok, Thailand, had developed. All the dirt roads in Singapore were completely gone as it had become an ultra-modern city, and the open drainage ditches in Tokyo were also gone.

My children enjoyed living in the Philippines. One of their favorite activities was watching the monkeys in the trees next to the house where we lived.

After a year we returned to the U.S. and settled in Dayton, Ohio. I commuted to work in Memphis, Tennessee, where I flew as a Second Officer in the DC-10 and then transitioned to the MD-11 as a First Officer. I chose to commute so that the family could be in a stable environment throughout their high school and college years. During my Air Force career, my wife and I had moved seven times and that was enough.

In 2000, besides flying for FedEx, I founded Synerbotics, a start-up company that combined nanotechnology with biotechnology to design advanced medical devices. My Chief Technology Officer was Dr. Tom Wailes, one of my classmates from the United States Air Force Academy class of 1977. He is an excellent scientist and highly skilled in computer science and electrical engineering. Our team also included gastroenterologists from the Dayton Children's Hospital. Synerbotics won the first phase of a business plan competition in 2002 sponsored by the i-Zone in Dayton, Ohio. In 2011, in light of changes in the marketplace, Synerbotics was discontinued.

After flying for ten years at FedEx, I became a Captain in the MD-11 and flew out of Anchorage, Alaska for several years before returning to fly out of Memphis. During my last three years at FedEx, all the children had graduated from college and were pursuing their careers. The time had come for Donna and I to consider where we wanted to settle in for our "empty nest" chapter. One of my FedEx pilot friends, Walt Reep, who lives on a ranch in Fallon, Nevada, urged us to consider Reno.

It didn't take us long to decide that was a great idea. While house hunting, I discovered that my 1977 Air Force Academy classmate, Rick

Sowers, also lives in Reno, and he was a big help in our search. Later I found out that there were several other Air Force Academy classmates I knew who also lived here, not the least of whom is John Reed. The last time John and I had crossed paths was twenty-five years earlier in the Pentagon when we both were assigned there by the Air Force.

The majestic mountains and the bright sunshine seen daily are some of the reasons we like Reno. We also enjoy the arid climate and almost hidden features of the high desert landscape such as the wildflowers that bloom in the spring adding a vast array of color to the usually brown sagebrush and sand, and the changing shapes of shadows cast upon the many mountain ranges as the sun traverses the sky from sunup to sundown. Also, we like that when it snows the snow doesn't normally hang around. That is, normally....

In 2017 I retired from FedEx satisfied that my flying for them had worked out so well.

One of my early activities after moving to Reno was assisting at the Innovation Center created by the University of Nevada. The purpose of the center is to assist entrepreneurs who are starting their own companies and companies that had not operated for very long be successful. I was able to share my own experience of running a nanotechnology business for eleven years, and I met several outstanding individuals during this time.

Reno hosts plenty of activities, including the National Championship Air Races, a major annual September event. This unique happening attracts visitors from all over the world. Shortly after we moved I made my first Air Races visit and ran into another classmate from the Air Force Academy, Kevin Roll. I found out that he races in the jet class in the Reno Air Races.

He invited me over to the jet racers' tent, where I met several people, one of whom was Rick Vandam, a 1973 Air Force Academy graduate, whose brother Dave was not only my Academy classmate, but was also a member of the 21st Squadron with me.

Instantly, Reno became home!

Because I met Kevin which led me to the others, I eventually became involved in working for the Reno Air Race Association for four years, serving as the Director of Flight Operations/Race Director, or

Air Boss, for the last two. What a great experience. My appreciation of all that comes with airplanes and piloting continues unabated although a whole new frontier of public service opened up and drew me in.

Following my stint with the Reno Air Races, I ran in 2022 for the office of Nevada Lieutenant Governor. I ran because I wanted to use my leadership skills to help improve how the state operates. Although I won thirteen out of the seventeen Nevada counties, I ended up getting edged out in the Primary by 5.8 percent. I learned a great deal running for this office, and it was well worth the hard work. The overall very positive response from Nevadans humbled me.

> The success described in this Chapter that I've experienced in my life is a direct result of the values that my parents raised me with and were essential to the foundation of my family. My Uncle Gordon and Grandmother Grady reinforced them. It's important to pass on our values. Ronald Reagan, in his January 5, 1967, inaugural address as California Governor said that freedom is only one generation away from extinction. I hold this to be true. And the reason it's only one generation away is because of our values. The measure of a country is determined by what its citizens value. Citizens act according to what they believe in; in what they value. Values are taught, absorbed, and reinforced by our environment while we grow and mature. The values that my parents imparted to me were Virtue, Strength of Character, Liberty, and Faith. These are my compasses that navigate me successfully through life. By describing some of my experiences, I hope to convey the importance of these values and the impact they can make.

# 3
# VIRTUE

*"We will not lie, steal, or cheat, nor tolerate among us anyone who does."*
The *Honor Code* originally established by cadets of the
first graduating class,

**United States Air Force Academy, 1959.**

Learning to be virtuous is an exceedingly worthwhile thing to do. Webster's defines virtue as general moral excellence, the right action, the right thinking, goodness, or morality. One of the hardest lessons that young people need to learn is that telling the truth, being honest, is essential. Another virtue is to have integrity. Perseverance is a virtue that stands out because it belongs to those who reach the finish line when others have long quit and left the race. Being thrifty is important because this virtue is the right action of living within your means. These are all virtues that my parents taught me and more importantly, they demonstrated these virtues by living them. Notably, these virtues are American values, values on which our country was built and values that are necessary to sustain it as a place of freedom into the future.

## HONESTY

While I lived in Philadelphia I attended the Joseph Pennell Elementary School, a public school located in the city's Belfield neighborhood. Pennell educated students from kindergarten through sixth grade at that time. One day while in fifth grade, my teacher discovered that I had cheated. So, she contacted my parents. I was very worried about what would happen to me at home later that day. This was a time when there was great respect between teachers and parents, when parents trusted teachers to uphold the values that were taught in the home and trusted they would not act as agents of the state who would undermine the family (as unfortunately is very common in public schools today).

Very nervous, I walked up our front steps to enter our house.

My father met me at the front door which led into our living room. As we stood there looking at each other he was quiet for what seemed like a very long time. When he began to speak, he told me to sit down in one of the living room chairs. He sat in a chair directly in front of me that he pulled over. He then asked me if what my teacher had reported, that she'd caught me cheating, was true. When I replied that it was, he said, "Let me tell you a story about why you shouldn't cheat."

He began by saying that there was a man who, when he was a boy, cheated in school. He cheated in elementary school and received good marks, he cheated in high school and received good marks, and he cheated in college which resulted in marks so good that he graduated with flying colors.

As my Dad spoke each part of the list of ways the man cheated, I became more anxious.

"And it turned out the man wanted to become a doctor, so he applied and was admitted to medical school," Dad said and then paused. At this point I wondered where the story was going. The cheating man seemed to be getting good results, but that couldn't be right. "He cheated there, too, of course. He would write the answers on the inside of the cuff of his shirt sleeve and look at them during the exams to find the answers to questions he didn't know," Dad continued, adding, "After medical school he became a practicing doctor."

Then the story went on since the man getting to be a doctor evidently wasn't the end.

Dad talked about one particular day when the man was on call to take care of any emergencies that might come into the hospital, and the nurse suddenly announced there was a patient in the emergency room that needed his immediate attention. He hurried to that part of the hospital to help the patient, of course. "And," said Dad, "when he arrived in the emergency room, he saw his mother lying on the table in front of him. She was unconscious and in critical condition."

I was shocked by this revelation. I couldn't imagine how awful it must have been for the man seeing his own mother like that. I listened intently as Dad explained how after examining his mother, the man who was now a doctor decided what procedure he needed to perform. However, things went wrong when he started working on his mother because he realized that he didn't know how to perform the procedure.

What a horrible thing for me to contemplate as Dad finished the story by emphasizing that since the man had cheated on his exams and couldn't remember what he needed to do to perform the procedure, his mother had died on the operating table. Even though he was a doctor, the man couldn't save her life.

Then Dad said, "Tony, it is very important that you don't cheat because it will catch up with you when you least expect it. Cheating is not the right thing to do." My father shared this story with me to get me to recognize that the value of being honest was very important and a foundational value in our family, and it stuck in my mind even until today. It is good to be taught this value at a young age, as I was.

When I was older, I joined the Boy Scouts of America. Being honest was something that the Boy Scouts called for in the first point of the Scout Law. Reciting "A Scout is trustworthy," along with the other eleven points of the Scout Law in unison with the other Scouts every week also helped to shape the habit of telling the truth and eventually instilled within me the desire to value being honest.

I can appreciate now how learning to be honest prepared me to attend the United States Air Force Academy where the Honor Code stated at that time, "We will not lie, steal or cheat nor tolerate anyone among us who does." After four years of living under the Honor Code at the Air Force Academy, I then became an Air Force pilot.

I remember an instance during Undergraduate Pilot Training when a few of my fellow classmates were having a spirited disagreement. I was sitting a few rows back from them. I looked up and commented that one of the guys had the right answer. The others immediately shouted, "Grady you're wrong, what do you know anyway?" Typical response for young males in their twenties full of testosterone competing against each other. I returned to what I was looking at without responding.

Simultaneously, another classmate from the other side of the room announced, "If Grady said it, that's the answer. I believe him. I don't trust any of you other guys." His comment silenced everyone, and the room quieted down.

I didn't really think much about this incident until many years later while in the heat-of-battle of raising my own children. I was also a Scoutmaster and an assistant high school track coach and dealt with many high-spirited young people, especially boys. I began to realize how odd it was for my pilot training classmate to come to my defense after my credibility was questioned by the others. This classmate was not particularly a friend. Many times, he tended to single me out in a group to announce my latest folly to the group. And I had many follies... however, when recalling this, it dawned on me that the value of honesty was part of me and could be seen by others, even back then at that time in my life when I was young.

Honesty is actually essential to safe flying. It is very important that a pilot is honest when writing any comments in the maintenance log at the end of the flight; otherwise, he could jeopardize the life of anyone who might fly after him. The maintenance people can only fix the problems they are aware of.

Bucking the current trend toward dishonesty is important and the virtue of honesty must be taught and passed on to the American generations to come.

## INTEGRITY

Honesty overlaps with integrity. If you tell the truth, you're honest. This is a good thing. However, integrity is something more. It means that you have the right conduct, that you are upright. If we think of a metal beam, we would say that the beam has integrity if it holds up after something hard hits it, yet the beam remains intact or stays together and doesn't break. So, a person has integrity if he conducts himself in a way so as not to bend and or break in the face of the attacks of the world against him. The person remains whole.

The book of Proverbs in the Bible warns a young man of the danger of going along with the wicked when they encourage him to join them. If the young man does throw in his lot with them, he will eventually end up with a life of ruin which he will later regret, especially when he is old.

When a person has integrity, he stands on principle. Everyone else also knows where this person stands. He acts in a consistent way. Even though others may not agree with him, they will respect him because he has integrity. My father taught me that "my word is my bond," meaning that I must do what I promise. Following through on your word convinces others that you will deliver what you promise. Doing this is very important to having integrity.

Another key part of integrity is what you do when no one else is watching. It is doing the right thing because it is the right thing to do, and not performing for the crowd or for the purpose of gaining some reward. I learned integrity because of what my parents taught me and especially because it was reflected in their lives. Without exception, I always heard my father's coworkers praise him for his honesty and integrity. All of them thought highly of him.

This level of dependability was equally true for my mother. She was so trusted that many in the community asked her to lead their groups. As an example, she was elected to be the president of the parents' auxiliary, a group that assisted the board of directors of our high school in making decisions. They probably elected her to this position because her integrity gave her a very favorable standing in the community. She was well thought of and the other parents trusted her. On the other hand though, she just might have pursued the position so she could keep an eye on me...

Today's news is packed with reports of national leaders who have been shown to lack integrity. Policies and decisions made by people who lack integrity are not likely to be those that would strengthen our country. Re-establishing integrity as a required value for a candidate to earn a vote would go a long distance toward getting America back on track.

## PERSEVERANCE

As recounted in Chapter 1, my parents and my uncle were clearly examples of perseverance. Being Black, growing up in the segregated South where Democratic Party office holders specifically put laws in place to intentionally keep Blacks from progressing beyond a certain level in life, my parents and my uncle thrived, advanced, and excelled.

It wasn't easy for them, yet they never talked about being victims. They demonstrated how to overcome the obstacles that the Democrats specifically placed in their path. Thus, they taught me to do the same. They taught me how to become successful.

Both my parents persevered in education. In Chapter 1 I wrote of how my mother was willing to go to another state to work as she traveled along a path to a better education. Though when graduating from college she became a Licensed Practical Nurse (LPN) and served in the nursing profession for most of her adult life, she eventually earned a Bachelor of Arts degree in gerontology, the study of the aging process, in 1981.

Earning a bachelor's degree was one of her goals in life. She earned it at age fifty-nine, a time when most people are well past pursuing any college degrees. She wasn't. She persevered until she reached her goal. She was a life-long learner.

When Dad was ready to advance his education by seeking a master's degree, the state of Virginia did not have institutions of higher learning for Blacks due to segregation. He did not let that deter him. He entered a Master's program in the state of New York and the state of Virginia paid for it through this special program:

"Regulations Governing the Administration of An Act to Provide Equal Educational Facilities for Certain Persons Denied Admission to Virginia State Colleges, Universities and Institutions of Higher Learning" (Chapter 54, Acts of Assembly, 1940).

As mentioned in Chapter 1, my Uncle Gordon pursued his master's degree to improve himself when he couldn't find work as an engineer, which he was qualified to do.

Developing perseverance can be the difference between never achieving your goals and having the satisfaction and benefits that come with success. Defining yourself as a victim when obstacles appear (and they usually do) works against the kind of perseverance that made America strong.

## THRIFT

Thrift is an important value to embrace because improving economically or increasing buying power is what raises a person's standard of living. Advancing financially cannot be achieved through increasing debt, but requires doing without now so that a person can afford more later. My parents and my uncle taught me this out loud through their conversations with me, but more importantly practiced being thrifty throughout their lives. My sister and I greatly benefited from their disciplined approach to handling money.

One of the habits that my mother had was re-using plastic zip-loc bags by washing and rinsing them after what was stored in them was used up and placing the wet bags on the dishrack to dry. She also did this with aluminum foil. I suspect that this practice was a holdover from growing up in the Depression where there was scarcity throughout the entire country.

My dad taught me how to manage money through a process he set up when I wanted to buy a rather expensive item, an Asahi Pentax single lens reflex camera or SLR. The camera cost $108.00, which was a very large sum of money and would be the most expensive item that I would own at that time in my life.

I was starting my freshman year in high school and enjoyed taking pictures. I hoped to join the school yearbook staff as a photographer at some point in the future. When he found out that I wanted this camera, he suggested a plan to accomplish my goal. He agreed to give me half of the cost of the camera as a birthday gift, and I would pay for the rest of the camera in monthly installments. I had an allowance until I earned money working as a pool lifeguard.

Dad wrote a contract explaining the terms of our agreement that both of us signed. Attached to the contract was a monthly payment schedule where the months were listed along with a space next to each of them.

During this period my father worked in Vietnam, and since we couldn't live there because of the war, he would come to visit us in Thailand once a month for a week at a time. Fortunately, every two years we would take a month break and return to the United States as a family. Our family followed this routine from the time I arrived in Bangkok, in the middle of sixth grade, though graduating from high school. During Dad's monthly visit, he and I would sit down, he would take out the camera contract, and I would pay him the amount I owed for that month and record it. The contract lasted a year.

This exercise taught me how to be intentional and disciplined in buying items that were very expensive. I learned that I needed to determine if I could afford the item and plan on how I would pay for it. Also, since I paid for half of the camera, I had "skin in the game," which made me value the camera and take good care of it. I still own that camera.

Successfully completing this contract between my father and me set the stage for the purchase of a much more expensive item later in life. At the end of my junior year at the United States Air Force Academy I looked forward to buying a car which we were not allowed to own until we were seniors.

Since I'd graduated from high school in Bangkok, Thailand, at seventeen, I was not allowed to drive. A person could not obtain an international driver's license in Thailand until age eighteen. So, this would be the first car that I ever owned.

Planning ahead, my parents set up a trust fund when I was younger to help pay for part of my college tuition. Because I had the fortunate opportunity to attend the Air Force Academy, my parents did not have to pay any tuition since all service academies including West Point,

Annapolis, the Coast Guard, and Merchant Marine Academies, are federally funded. Dad let me know that on my twenty-first birthday the ownership of the trust fund would transfer to me. I decided that I wanted to use this gracious gift from my parents to buy my first car.

Like most cadets I wanted a sports car. I decided to buy a Datsun 280Z. There was one slight problem though with my plan. Since I entered the Air Force Academy at seventeen, I wouldn't turn twenty-one until December, six months after I graduated. That meant I could not use the trust fund to buy my car for my senior year at the Air Force Academy. To solve this problem, I asked my father for a no interest loan to buy my car and I would pay him back when the trust fund transferred to me and he agreed to the plan.

The 280Z cost $6,000.00, which was amazingly expensive at the time, but less than a Chevrolet Corvette, which several of my other classmates purchased. The Datsun 280Z and Chevrolet Corvette were very popular cars with members of the Air Force Academy Class of 1977, my class.

Dad helped me buy my car because he trusted me to follow through. That December when I was a Second Lieutenant attending Air Force Undergraduate Pilot Training at Williams Air Force Base in Chandler Arizona, I paid my father back as promised.

Dad was teaching me to be thrifty through helping buy my camera and through helping me when I bought my first car. Because he was willing to give me a no interest loan, I was able to buy the car I wanted for the lowest cost. I was not burdened with paying any interest on a loan.

Money management and sound budgeting, both integral to thrift, were important lessons for me to learn and set me firmly on the path of understanding how to handle all my future financial decisions.

> Being honest, having integrity, persevering and demonstrating thriftiness were all virtues that my parents and my uncle exhibited in their lives and taught me to value. These virtues are keys to my success in life and keys to a successful and thriving America as well.

# 4
# STRENGTH OF CHARACTER

*"A man must stand erect, not be kept erect by others."*
—**Marcus Aurelius,** *Meditations*

My grandmother, father, mother, and Uncle Gordon Grady all had tremendous strength of character. This American value is captured in the familiar saying, "When the going gets tough, the tough get going." They all certainly kept going in their lives, seeking education, working as professionals, and raising families. Through pursuing goals in each of these areas of their lives, they made lasting impressions on everyone around them in a positive way.

Most importantly their lives helped to shape who I am. Their example as well as those of others taught me the value of hard work and individual responsibility, being deliberate and taking responsibility for my actions. These traits work together to give a person strength of character. Upon reflection, I can readily see how the impact of these influences helped me obtain the leadership positions I've been fortunate enough to hold throughout my life.

## Lessons, Part 1

Steve Prefontaine (1951-1975) was one of the greatest distance runners in the world. He ran on the University of Oregon track team and set records in the 2,000- and 10,000-meter races. As the assistant track and field coach, I had the privilege of training my oldest son in track, working under the very able hand of Coach Phil Scott, the head coach for Dayton Christian high school in Dayton, Ohio. Phil himself was a world class athlete as a decathlon Olympic Trials qualifier.

Coach Scott told stories about Steve Prefontaine, especially when the athletes under our care would complain about the difficulty of practicing consistently. Phil shared that Steve Prefontaine's records would probably someday be broken, except for one. When Prefontaine prepared for the 1972 Olympics, he had a perfect training record. He never missed a day of practice during those entire four years. This record can only be equaled.

Phil used Prefontaine's dedication to practice to show the high school athletes that hard work rewarded those who were committed to follow through. This kind of lesson is one reason that I encourage young people to participate in sports. Sports develops the discipline to work hard, which instills a solid work ethic in athletes, which benefits many other aspects of their lives.

## Lessons, Part 2

We lived in several places in Philadelphia. In the beginning we lived in a house with other members of our extended family. Then our branch of the family moved into an apartment. Finally, my parents were able to purchase a two-story row house, where the sidewalls were attached to the house next to our house on both sides. All the houses lined up in a row up and down the street. Row houses are very common in the city of Philadelphia.

After living in the house for a short while, my parents decided to improve the house by removing the wallpaper and painting the inside of the house. With his industrial arts training, my father was well suited for this task. He was a skilled painter. The work began with everyone in our immediate family, my dad, mom, sister, and me all pitching in. We started in the living room located on the first floor of the house. We first had to strip the wallpaper from all the walls.

This process turned out to be very involved, requiring long hours and tedious work. Dad used the steam from boiling water in a steam pot on our stove and some other special tools. The steam softened the glue holding the wallpaper on the wall, and the tools made it possible for dad to remove large strips of wallpaper. Removing the wallpaper using steam protected the wall from damage. It was very important because it greatly reduced the amount of preparation that Dad would need to do later to prepare the wall surface for painting.

There were about four layers of wallpaper. I thought we would never finish the job. The clumps of stripped wallpaper fell to the floor and piled up as my dad diligently worked. My job was to pick up as much of the pile as I could at a time by gathering it in a box. Then I would carry the box through the front door, down the steps in the vestibule, through the storm door, outside, down another set of steps to a large trashcan on one side, clear of the walkway that led up to the house. Once there I would empty the box.

Making multiple trips back and forth to the trashcan became very boring for a nine-year-old little boy. Carrying heavy box loads was very tiring. One night in the middle of this process, I gave out because I was so tired. I decided to go upstairs and hide in my bedroom. Noticing my box in the middle of the floor and watching me walk up the stairs, Dad called out, "Hey buddy, where are you going?" He always called me buddy when he was about to teach me something.

I told him I was tired and that I was done. He explained to me that I need to put in a full day's work on the job, and that he was depending on me to do my part. He knew that the "lazies" were coming out in me and causing me to want to give up. He coaxed me back, and I continued to carry the box loads of stripped wallpaper to the trashcan.

This incident is the first time I can remember that I pushed myself to do something I really didn't want to do because my father encouraged me to do so. This lesson was extremely important for me to learn and came in handy later in life when quitting something couldn't be an option.

Sometimes it can seem as if everything worth doing requires that you go well past your point of fatigue to complete the task. When working a job for someone who is paying you, it is important to complete the work you promised when you agreed to complete it. The strips of wallpaper lesson contributed to my strength of character by helping me understand the respect and sense of satisfaction that comes from working hard and being dependable. This foundation helped me develop as a solid high school athlete and later to become a good Division I track & field athlete at the Air Force Academy. I earned a letter competing in the high jump and triple jump.

## **LESSONS, PART 3**

Another time I was made keenly aware of the value of strength of character was through the actions of one of the members of the Protestant Youth Group that met on Carswell Air Force Base. I was the Youth Director at that time. The group decided to go on a ski trip in New Mexico one year. To raise funds to finance the trip they came up with the idea of holding a series of car washes and bake sales on the Air Force Base. They planned to hold these activities for a six-month period.

The agreement was made that the money they raised would be spread amongst the youth group members. The goal was to raise enough money to pay for half of each member's trip, and that each youth would then be responsible for the rest of the cost. They worked hard and very well together as a team to achieve this goal, and they were successful.

A few weeks before the trip several members of the group informed me that Sally[47], one of the members of the group, worked as hard if not harder than everyone else and was present at every event. However, though the funds they raised would pay for half of everyone's trip, she could not afford to pay for the other half, and wouldn't be able to join them.

They wanted her to go, so they all decided to chip in and make that possible. All the youth appreciated Sally and thought her perfect attendance record of helping with all the fundraising events earned her a spot on the trip.

I thought it was a great idea! I was very impressed that high school students would be so thoughtful. Just maybe all those Bible principles were starting to sink in, especially the one about "love your neighbor as yourself."[48] I spoke with Sally and shared with her what the other members of the group said and stressed that they really wanted her to go with them.

I congratulated Sally on her perfect record of working at all the fundraising events to encourage her to accept the offer the others made. But Sally looked at me squarely in the eye and said, "It is very kind that they want me to go on the trip. I feel honored that they would try to do this for me; however, this is a kind of charity, and my family does not accept charity."

Sally was being raised by a single mom and I'm sure money was very tight. I'm also sure her mom was striving as hard as she could to provide. Though the rest of the group was disappointed, Sally stood firm in her refusal. It took great strength of character for Sally to handle the situation in the very mature manner she did and to make certain her mom didn't feel hurt in some way.

## LESSONS, PART 4

My mother taught me to look at the person I'm talking with squarely in the eye.

Both of my parents made sure I spoke clearly and loudly enough to be heard. They stressed that I should stand tall and present myself because I had nothing to fear or to be ashamed of. It was part of the culture of the segregated South that second-class citizens were not to look at their self-proclaimed "superiors" in the eye. The Democratic Party public office holders practiced subjugating Blacks who the Party stated were inferior.

Standing tall, looking the person I was talking to straight in the eye, and giving a firm handshake are how my parents taught me to act. Conducting myself in this way has served me well in how I present myself when speaking with other people. Because of this practice others have no problem hearing me. They may not particularly like what I say, but they hear me very clearly. And that is a good thing because when I address others, I have something to say, and I want to make sure they hear it whether they may want to or not. Straightforwardness helps establish presence which is a contributor to the value of strength of character.

## OBSERVATIONS, PART 1

As a freshman in high school, I held my first elected office. At that time, the International School of Bangkok (ISB) had a Student Supreme Court that would work with the Dean of Students to determine if the school's Constitution was being upheld. A student justice was elected from each class and, in addition to the senior class justice, another senior served as the chief justice of the entire court. The Dean of Students advised the court as well as represented the faculty and also served as the representative for the Principal and the Superintendent.

I learned much from the upperclassmen who served on the court. Participating in the court really gave me an insight into how differing interpretations give rise to questions about rules and regulations, and how these questions are answered. The court also served as an outlet for the student body to voice their opinions to the faculty in an orderly and formal way.

After serving on the Student Supreme Court my freshman year, I was later elected Class President for my sophomore, junior, and senior years. I enjoyed running these campaigns. Taking part in competitions between the classes taught me how to plan and to figure out what strengths and weaknesses other classmates might have.

At our school the junior class was responsible for planning and hosting the Junior-Senior Prom. Raising money was always a challenge, especially for the Prom. We held various activities like bake sales. These were a frequent and very reliable fundraising activities thanks to many volunteers, especially Michelle Chan and her team. They would respond to my distressed request for help, often the night before, along with Mimi Drake, who was elected Class Secretary during our sophomore year.

Mimi and I worked together solving problems that involved many class issues. And still today in 2023, Mimi is the great organizer of activities that have helped members of the ISB Class of 1973 maintain contact through the years, even though members of the class live in countries all over the world. The most innovative fundraising activity though, was our fashion show. It was a blast and raised quite a bit of money.

I was glad to be Class President, and I was humbled by the trust that my fellow students placed in me year after year. Without the wisdom I'd gained from family and other experiences, I doubt that I would have been elected. Strength of character and leadership skills go hand in hand.

## OBSERVATIONS, PART 2

Of course, attending school as a guest in a foreign country is not without its problems. During the late sixties and early seventies there were many problems in Thailand which, at times, involved students from the ISB. One of those problems was the use of illegal drugs. These drugs were quite easy to obtain in Bangkok.

Unfortunately, one day the *Bangkok Post*, a major newspaper, featured an article that condemned and suggested that most of the students attending ISB used drugs and were not very nice people. The title of the article was "Drug Squad to Watch ISB." The Stars and Stripes, a newspaper with a very wide circulation throughout Asia, and AP (Associated Press) also published the information from this article. It caused quite a stir within the international community, especially among the parents in Bangkok and throughout the rest of Asia. But during this dark time, one of the ISB faculty members wrote a thoughtful and powerful rebuttal[49] to the accusations made in the article in a Letter to the Editor.

The faculty member was Robert Kovach, a biology teacher and one of the school's basketball coaches. He wrote that there were too many generalities listed in the article that did not apply to most of the students. He agreed that there were some students who attended the school who did take drugs, and about how he had personally turned in three of his students for this offense.

Moreover, he commented, "ISB students are Great!", referring to the high character of most of the students who attended ISB. As examples he listed the names of twelve students. One of them was me.

I was surprised to see my name listed in print in the newspaper. I was also honored that Mr. Kovach had such high opinion of me, especially since I never quite lived up to his standards to be selected for the school basketball team (which I tried out for every year...).

What strikes me most now about Mr. Kovach selecting students he judged as "Great," is that he was recognizing the strength of character of those students. Developing strength of character and earning the respect of others can be a strong incentive to be the best person you can be.

## **OBSERVATIONS, PART 3**

After a long, arduous climb my eight-member patrol finally reached the top. We were exhausted. The impenetrable blackness of the starless night sky was quiet and eerie. It was cold. We could see hardened lava rocks only a few feet in each direction surrounding us illuminated by the faint narrow beams of our flashlights. As patrol leader I instructed everyone to bed down for the night. We shed our packs, erected our tents, unrolled our sleeping bags, crawled in, and zipped up. During the strangeness of this environment, once inside the familiar comfort of our warm cocoons we drifted off into a sound sleep.

At sunrise we were awakened by the sun's radiance illuminating the bright brilliant blue sky. The air was crisp and clear. There we were. Everyone was accounted for. We stood in awe of this breathtaking view. Yesterday's hard climb was now well worth it. We'd done it! We stood at sunrise on the top of Mount Fuji. It was August, 1971, at the 13th World Jamboree held in Asagiri Heights, Japan. I was fifteen.

This triumph and other events were typical of my Boy Scouting experiences that greatly influenced my life. Such activities along with attaining the rank of Eagle Scout helped me by incentivizing me to pay attention to the kind of man I should want to be. I know being a Boy Scout contributed to me eventually attending the United States

Air Force Academy and serving my country as an active-duty Air Force pilot for the next twenty years.

I had many leadership opportunities in the organization, first learning to become a good follower, and later leading the troop of about one hundred boys as the Senior Patrol Leader and reaching the highest rank of Eagle Scout.

When I was recommended for Eagle Scout, my Scoutmaster, Preston E. Law, Jr., attached a personal note to my mother to the recommendation letter that he wrote to Eagle Board of Review and the Far East Council Executives. In that note he mentioned that I was only the fourth boy that he had ever recommended for the rank of Eagle Scout in the six years he served as Scoutmaster.[50]

Still more importantly, later in life scouting inspired me to serve my community as Scoutmaster from 2006 until 2008 for Troop 71, sponsored by Aley United Methodist Church in Beavercreek, Ohio.

I became Scoutmaster because the current Scoutmaster, Pat Price, who had served in this position for six years, asked me to take over for him. It's never easy to take on such an important job, not to mention I was an airline pilot at that time and always on the move.

Already a member of the Troop Committee, I just knew I didn't have enough time to take on such an important position. My two boys had benefited from Scouting, with the youngest well established on the trail to Eagle at that time.

Then, deep within me, the Spirit of Scouting welled up and recalled all the men who had put their shoulders to the plough when they didn't have the time and served as Boy Scout leaders when I was a youth. They dedicated themselves to my growth and development as well as all the other boys they led in Scouting. With their encouragement, I earned the rank of Eagle Scout which I proudly wore as a youth. In that moment I knew it was my turn, and I took the reins.

A Scoutmaster encounters a great number of boys. At the end of my time serving as Scoutmaster I was awarded the Scoutmaster Award of merit by the National Eagle Scout Association[51]. The strength of character that Scouting helped to develop in me ended up bringing benefits to both myself and the Scouting program.

## OBSERVATIONS, PART 4

Attending College at the United States Air Force Academy was my goal. The institution was a perfect fit for me. With rigorous academics, demanding physical requirements, and the honor to be developed into the next generation of officers that would serve in the United States Air Force. Attending the Academy was a priceless opportunity for me.

Naturally, the Air Force Academy wanted well-rounded students. The course of study did not allow for sitting back and taking it easy. I majored in Astronautical Engineering, or Astro, as it was affectionately called. In this field students studied the theories and principles involved in space flight. Astro was one of the more difficult majors at the Air Force Academy.

I survived the course of study under the outstanding instruction given by the faculty members of the Department of Astronautics and Computer Science. One professor, Lieutenant Colonel Edward D. Merkl, was especially noteworthy. Doc Merkl, as we called him, was a true gentleman. Having grown up in Alabama, he had a distinct southern drawl. His warm smile added to his easy-going nature. He held a PhD in electrical engineering. Also, he was a Test Pilot and a graduate of the United States Air Force Test Pilot School located at Edwards Air Force Base in Southern California.

Doc Merkl was a member of the Air Force's Manned Orbital Laboratory (MOL) Program, where the Air Force intended to put men in space. The program was eventually scrubbed. So, Doc Merkl had a wealth of knowledge and experience to pass on to us, his Astro students. But our favorite part of the class was the beginning. Doc Merkl started every class with a joke, usually about an incident involving one of his fellow test pilots at Edwards Air Force Base. He held our attention as we listened intently.

Once, when going to his office to ask questions I noticed that Doc Merkl was organizing three-by-five cards in a box. The cards were neatly indexed. Curious, I asked about the box. He looked up and said that this was his box of jokes that he told in class, and that he made sure he didn't tell a joke more than once to each class section. I don't know how many sections he taught, but I'm sure with only about twelve students in each of our class sections, he probably taught at least four sections. His organization was impressive.

Under Doc Merkl's instruction, I set my sights on becoming an Air Force Test Pilot. During our senior year, Lieutenant Colonel Merkl would surprise us during various lab periods when he would secretly invite guest speakers to lecture instead of doing the work for that lab. The speakers were those with whom he'd flown at Edwards Air Force Base. They were the pilots we'd heard jokes about during our prior years of instruction as Astro majors. Many of them were now Air Force Generals who were in very influential positions making decisions that would determine the future of the Air Force. These lectures gave us tremendous insight into how advanced technology was researched and eventually applied in the Air Force.

Our least favorite part of the class was taking notes. All the classrooms in Fairchild Hall, the academic building at the Air Force Academy, were set back from the outside walls of the building, so there were no windows in any of the walls. Instead, the four walls were covered with white boards. Doc Merkl would reel us in with his slow-talking southern drawl as he began writing on the upper left-hand corner of the whiteboard in the front of the classroom. He wrote almost continuously as he taught us, and moved until he filled all the white boards in the classroom by the end of class. He wrote much faster than he talked. We had to keep up! Also, when solving equations, he came up with the answers in his head much faster than we could on our calculators. He was a product of the generation of engineers who used the slide-rule[52] to solve problems.

There were two courses of study in the Astro major: spacecraft design and feed-back control theory. Each student chose one as their major field of study. I chose feed-back control theory, which is the field of science used to determine how to position rocket motors and control surfaces on an airborne vehicle like a rocket, to make sure it follows the intended navigation path or flight path. These principles are used to determine the flying-qualities, or how well an airplane flies, as it responds when the pilot moves the airplane's controls.

Another major area of instruction at the Air Force Academy was in military training. We were taught the essential elements of leadership.

During the freshman year, cadets are taught how to follow well. As the cadet advances through the years, more opportunities become available to lead at various levels. The Cadet Wing was planned to consist of four thousand cadets. There are forty squadrons with each made up of one hundred cadets. There are various jobs for the members of each class year in the squadron, with the seniors in the most influential leadership positions.

One of the more popular time periods for leadership at the Air Force Academy is training the incoming new cadets during what is called basic training, or Beast, as we liked to call it. This takes place in the summer before the start of the academic year to transition the new cadets from their former life into cadet life. During Beast, there are ten squadrons of one hundred new or basic cadets.

I had the privilege of serving as squadron commander for one of those squadrons. At the end of basic training, I was voted by my peers, the nine other seniors who served as squadron commanders, as the Outstanding Basic Squadron Commander. The institution had no input in this decision. To win this award from my fellow seniors was very meaningful to me.

In my senior year, the Air Force Academy chose me to appear on the cover of the recruitment brochure. This selection showed that the academy viewed me as a good example for those considering attending the Air Force Academy, and was an honor for me.

The 1977 United States Air Force Academy Recruiting Brochure.
From left to right: Kim Martini a Fourth Classman (Freshman), Mark Swigonski a Second Classman (Junior), and Tony Grady a First Classman (Senior).
Mark and I were members of Cadet Squadron 21.
Kim was a member of Cadet Squadron 3.

At graduation, recognizing my military performance over my four years as a cadet, I was given the award for the Cadet Who Best Exemplifies the Highest Ideals of Loyalty, Integrity, and Courage, sponsored by the Family and Friends of Major General John K. Hester, in his memory.[53] Among many accomplishments, he was a "Flying Tigers" Distinguished Flying Cross recipient.[54] I was honored that this award was presented to me by Virginia Hester Wooddell, daughter of General Hester, and my parents were there to witness this occasion.[55]

There is no doubt in my mind that my receiving these awards is a direct reflection of the strength of character my parents instilled in me while growing up.

## OBSERVATIONS, PART 5

After I was no longer a cadet, my experiences as an Air Force pilot continued to illustrate the solid grounding I'd received along the way to that point. Graduating from the United States Air Force Test Pilot School qualified me as an experimental test pilot, capable of accomplishing what is called Developmental Tests. These tests are performed on experimental, or brand-new airplanes. The various jobs that I held once I entered the field of testing airplanes eventually prepared me to be given the command of the 420th, the B-2 Test and Evaluation, squadron.

One of these jobs was leading the combined test force that conducted the selection of the Air Force's newest training aircraft in 1989: the T-1A Jayhawk. Another position that helped me along the way was working in the Pentagon from 1993 to 1995 at the United States Air Force Headquarters on the Air Staff. In this job, I was responsible for writing the bomber section of the Air Force's part of the U.S. President's budget. I was also involved with the overall management of the Air Force bomber force.

In 1993, I was assigned as the Operations Officer, or 'flying boss', for the B-2 Test squadron; and in June 1996, I was selected to command the squadron. Flying the B-2 Stealth Bomber was the high point of my Air Force flying career.

To make test operations as safe as possible, when the B-2 flew a test mission, it was accompanied by a chase aircraft. Pilots flying in the chase aircraft would help look for other aircraft that might interfere with test operations and observe the test aircraft to make sure nothing unusual developed with the airplane.

Most of the chase aircraft pilots were also test pilots qualified in the B-2, so on many occasions they would offer suggestions when asked by the crew inside the B-2 flying a test mission to solve problems that occurred. The F-16 and the T-38 aircraft were used for this purpose.

All the pilots in the squadron, in addition to being qualified in the B-2, were also qualified in the F-16 or the T-38. My second qualification was in the F-16, which was a pleasure to fly. During the test program I flew many first flights, or a flight where a particular event was tried for the first time in the airplane.

One of my favorite first flights was the release of eighty Mk-82 low drag bombs from the airplane. The Mk-82 is a five-hundred-pound general purpose bomb. I had the opportunity to fly this flight with my Air Force Academy classmate Steve Cameron on June 28, 1996. At that time, he commanded the squadron, and I was the operations officer.

The flight went flawlessly. This flight was also important because the B-2 was only the second bomber that could drop 80 Mk-82 bombs at the same time. In the past, the B-52D, a Vietnam era bomber, was the only aircraft capable of dropping that many bombs at one time. But since that airplane was retired in 1983[56] the capability of dropping this large number of bombs was missing until the B-2 bomber became part of the Air Force arsenal of combat aircraft. I retired from the Air Force after twenty years, two weeks after the B-2 reached its initial combat capability, or was ready for use in combat.

When preparing to launch on a test mission, there are many items that must be done and checked on the ground before takeoff, as with any airplane. This process takes much longer in a test airplane and is quite involved.

During my last flight in the B-2, while in the middle of accomplishing these checks, the test director, who was sitting in the test room with the engineers that monitor all the aircraft systems, called me over the radio and said, "Tony, look out of your window."

I did.

All the members of the squadron and the rest of the test force organization who were not actively involved in the test mission that day were lined up in front of the test force buildings across the ramp from my airplane waving at me. They all knew it was my last flight in the B-2, and they came out to say goodbye.

I must say this send-off took me by surprise, and I thought about what a privilege it was to command such an outfit and how this would be among my most memorable moments in my Air Force career. It was an honor to lead the men and women of the 420th Flight Test Squadron at Edwards Air Force Base.

Without my having technical competence and a demonstrated ability to lead, the United States Air Force wouldn't have assigned me to command such an outstanding and important organization. Because of the American value of strength of character that my parents instilled in me as I grew up, I had been given this extraordinary opportunity.

## OBSERVATIONS, PART 6

After retiring from the Air Force, I was hired by FedEx. Married with four small children, I knew I needed to work for a solid company that would allow me to provide for the needs of my family. My wife and I worked hard to instill in our children the values that we were raised with and to guide them to seek their own profession through obtaining a college education.

I chose to fly for FedEx because this company was the leader in flying cargo around the world and throughout the United States. Fred Smith, one of the most forward-thinking CEOs of the 20th and the 21st centuries, started the company.

I was fascinated with how the idea for FedEx came to Smith during his time attending Yale University. His business professor was not impressed when he submitted his idea for one of the required assignments.[57] He was given an average grade, or "C", on the paper.[58] It is a good thing Smith's strength of character kept him from being discouraged by the 'know-it-all' academic. I'll take the guy with the "C" who produces something over those with their academic theories who never have to produce anything worthwhile in the practical world.

## OBSERVATIONS, PART 7

Helping me to make the decision to work for FedEx were my 1977 United States Air Force Academy classmate, Terry Fennessy, and J.D. Seal, a 1981 graduate of the Academy who worked for me while I was stationed at the Pentagon. When I called Terry to ask about working for FedEx, he simply replied, "Tony, in an economically up market, FedEx makes money; in an economically down market, FedEx makes money."

He paused and became silent. Terry was my Astronautical Engineer lab partner at the Academy and he knew me well. He waited until his very simple but profound comment sunk in. When we'd worked together, J.D. often talked about how much time he was able to spend with his daughter, supporting her in the various activities she participated in, and was able to do this because he worked for FedEx.

I applied and was hired by the company. I'm sure one of the essential reasons why FedEx hired me was that my last boss in the Air Force, Col. Stuart L. Haupt, wrote a letter highly recommending me.[59] I view his high regard for me as a direct result of the value of strength of character that my parents worked tirelessly to make an important part of me.

For FedEx, I was first domiciled in Subic Bay in the Republic of the Philippines, which was the original location for FedEx's Asian hub of operations. This assignment afforded our family with an opportunity to have wonderfully enriching experiences.

I flew trips all over the world and eventually became a Captain on the MD-11, a wide-body airplane. I especially enjoyed visiting Almaty, Kazakhstan, a former Soviet Union satellite state. I took Russian at the United States Air Force Academy, and although I was far from being able to carry on a conversation, my limited vocabulary was enough to make myself understood.

During my FedEx career I also served as an instructor and an evaluator. FedEx provided me various job opportunities, each requiring increased responsibilities. I will be forever grateful that my parents trained me to embrace strength of character; the company trusted me, and I represented them well.

## STRENGTH OF CHARACTER CLOSER TO THE HERE AND NOW

I retired from FedEx in 2017 and my wife and I settled down in Reno, Nevada. The high desert and majestic mountains attracted us along with the warm, friendly, and very welcoming people of Nevada. Seeing the bright sunshine and clear blue sky daily is very uplifting. The favorable climate does not become overly hot in the summer and usually involves a mild snowfall in the winter.

Though my relationship with Nevada began 42 years ago when I attended my first Red Flag[60] exercise held at Nellis Air Force Base, located in Las Vegas, we were made aware of Reno by one of my fellow FedEx pilots, Walt Reep, who is a rancher in Fallon, Nevada, located about an hour and a half from Reno. An unforeseen treat has been the opportunity to eat some of the beef that he and his wife, Kitty, have raised on their ranch. The taste of this fresh beef is much more delicious than the meat that I was used to buying in the grocery store as a city dweller.

Now that I was retired, I was looking forward to putting my feet up and taking it easy. And since Reno is the home of the National Championship Air Races, I decided that I needed to attend this event. I found the races very interesting.

During this first visit I ran into my Air Force Academy classmate, Kevin Roll. I had not seen him since graduation from the Academy. After catching up on the highlights of our lives since our Academy days, Kevin invited me over to the tent where the pilots who raced jets at the Air Races hung out. Kevin was one of the jet racers. As Kevin introduced me to the members of this organization called the jet racing class, I met Rick Vandam.

Much to my surprise, not only was Rick a 1973 graduate of the Air Force Academy, his brother Dave was in my class at the Academy and we were in the same squadron, the 21$^{st}$ Cadet Squadron. As it turned out, seven of my Air Force Academy classmates live in the Reno area, which is great.

I came to Reno thinking life was going to settle down from the hectic pace of a commuting airline pilot; little did I know that this slower pace would be short lived. A few months after our initial meeting, Rick Vandam let me know that the National Championship Reno Air Racing Association was looking for an Air Boss and asked if I would be interested in taking this position.

Not knowing what an Air Boss did, but being sure I could handle the job because it was an aviation job, I agreed. One must be careful what he agrees to. For the next four years I worked at the Air Races. I understudied the current Air Boss, Greg, "Shifty" Peairs for two years, and then took over for him for the next two years.

Shifty had served in this position for thirteen years. Since I didn't know anything about Air Racing, I had a steep learning curve in front of me. Learning the ins and outs of this operation was very stimulating. Essentially, the Air Boss plans and carries out the Air Race schedule and works with the seven different race organizations, or classes, to make sure the racing rules approved by the Federal Aviation Administration, or FAA, are followed.

Each racing class is defined by the type of airplane that races in the class. The seven classes are: Formula One, Bi Plane, T-6, Sport, Jet, Unlimited, and STOL/Drag.[61] Weaved in between the races are performances by demonstration airplanes. Finally, about every other year the Air Races hosts one of the military demonstration teams like the Air Force Thunderbirds or the Navy Blue Angels.

The airshows these teams put on are very popular, so the Air Boss orchestrates this week-long event. Though planning and carrying out this task requires quite a bit of work, in the end it is quite satisfying when all the of the events successfully come together.

Though the Reno Air Race Association chooses the Air Boss, the FAA must approve the individual who will fill this position. It was my privilege to serve the Reno community as the Director of Flight Operations, or Air Boss and Race Director, for the 2020 and 2021 National Championship Air Races. The 2020 races were eventually cancelled due to the COVID-19 Pandemic, but in 2021 the races were very successful.

Again, I believe it was the strength of character that not only the Reno Air Race Association saw in me, but also the FAA, that resulted in my selection as Air Boss. In great part I have my parents to thank for preparing me to be the kind of person who could fill such an important position.

> Strength of Character is a value that my parents were careful to develop in me as I was growing up. It is a value that greatly benefited me. It was the foundation for all of the leadership positions I had the privilege of filling throughout my life. It is a characteristic easy to recognize in the person who possesses it. Strength of Character is an American value that must be intentionally instilled in those who will come after us as they grow and develop.

# 5
# LIBERTY

*"Where there is no law, there is no liberty."*
—**Benjamin Rush,** *Founding Father who signed the U.S. Declaration of Independence*

Men seek liberty. In all places at all times in history, men seek liberty. Though related to freedom, liberty is freedom enjoyed within certain bounds. Freedom without bounds leads to anarchy. Liberty is the freedom to exercise self-control and not be controlled by someone else. Liberty is the personal freedom to work toward obtaining the goals you set for yourself. However, you cannot exercise personal freedom unless you live in an environment where exercising your freedom is encouraged and protected. This is the establishment of liberty for the citizens within a country.

The right to be free is one of the most basic values upon which our country was originally built. However, men cannot operate within a group if freedom is not checked. That freedom is bound by the rule of law to give all a chance to be equally free.

In 2006, a study was conducted to see how children would react in a playground with or without a fence around it. When taken to a playground without a fence, the children huddled around their teacher and would not move very far from her, or ever be out of her line-of-sight. When on the playground with the fence, the children ran about freely without a care all over the playground.[62]

This experiment demonstrated that the children felt safer when they could plainly see the boundary, the limit of where they could go, in contrast to how they reacted when there was no clear boundary. This outcome illustrates how freedom needs well-defined boundaries, and history shows that laws are what create these boundaries.

I believe that the type of laws that create the boundaries that unleash freedom come from a limited government, because the purpose of government is to form the boundaries of personal responsibility and not attempt to control every action of the citizen. The latter would result in tyranny. I also believe that the early history of the United States offers valuable insights into how the U.S. Constitution was written to both provide and safeguard liberty for this country.

## Historical /Political Background of Liberty in the United States

In the United States, the framework for these laws began when the country was founded on July 4, 1776, in the Declaration of Independence where it is clearly stated that liberty is a value second only to life; and in what Americans believe is an inalienable right, or a right given by God to which all men are entitled. Later, the Constitution of the United States became the supreme law of the land on March 4, 1789.[63]

The Founding Fathers viewed that rights do not come from governments, but from God who institutes governments; and that governments exist solely to protect the rights given to men by God. In explaining this important idea, Thomas Jefferson wrote, "The God who gave us life gave us liberty at the same time." We failed to live up to this value by not applying it to all Americans (a source of disagreement among the Founders that started at the beginning of the nation); the disagreement grew and eventually boiled up into a clash of ideas about how society should operate. This clash was one of the issues that caused the American Civil War.

It is important to realize though that, at the time of the country's founding, the slave trade was present all over the world. Specifically, the supply chain of the trade in flesh from Africa not only had European participants, but was established and flourished because of the Muslims in Arab lands, and the Africans who sold other Africans captured during tribal warfare. Therefore, the world environment at our nation's founding encouraged the terrible practice of slavery.

Though the problem of equality for all American citizens was not solved immediately after the Civil War, the country did purposely change direction regarding slavery since the ideal stated in the country's founding documents declared that all men are created equal. Therefore, the United States needed to start governing in that way. It was a long hard struggle to make this ideal a reality, but there has been continual improvement even though sometimes progress slowed to a crawl or even moved backwards.

However, since the end of the Civil War, the overall trend has moved in a positive direction. With the passing of the Thirteenth Amendment which ended slavery, the Fourteenth Amendment securing citizenship for those born in the United States especially former slaves, the Fifteenth Amendment allowing all males to vote, especially blacks, and the Nineteenth Amendment giving women the right to vote, the conduct of society moved closer to the ideal.

The Civil Rights movement in the 1950s and the 1960s purposed to end national discrimination against Blacks.[64] However, from the beginning as with the Civil War, the Democrats opposed moving forward toward equal opportunity for all in our country. They opposed it at the beginning of the Civil War and continued to oppose it with the implementation of Jim Crow laws when Reconstruction failed. The Southern States reverted to single party rule resulting in elected Black Republicans being voted out of office. So, gains made by Black Americans after the war quickly evaporated.

The South was governed in this manner for decades using such tactics as gerrymandering or the careful drawing of congressional districts, which made it extremely difficult to remove the incumbent ruling office holders who supported segregation. Though gerrymandering was first used in 1812 in Massachusetts, later it was specifically used by the Democrats in the South to keep Blacks from being elected to public office.[65]

In the recent 2022 election cycle, gerrymandering and the like continues, but the target now is defeating those who believe in American values and believe the rule of law comes from a limited government and oppose collectivism, where the ruling elite forces its will on the people. The result is imposed laws with which most people do not agree. A clear example of this is that according to a Monmouth poll conducted in 2021, 80% of the American people want voter ID to ensure the credibility of the election process[66].

Here in Nevada where I reside, an OH Insights poll conducted for the Nevada Independent Newspaper showed that 74% of Nevadans favor voter ID.[67] Yet every time legislation is introduced to make voter ID the law, the Democrat lawmakers both nationally and locally vote it down, demonstrating that they do not care about the will of the people that they claim to represent.

Fortunately, more Americans are waking up, realizing this is a problem, and are taking action to correct this serious situation. The Democrat collectivist world view is that our elected leaders should dictate by imposing their will on the people instead of serving by representing the will of the people.

Unfortunately, the use of tactics like gerrymandering and changing the laws that govern how elections are conducted are making it more difficult to remove and replace those who seek to latch on to and hold their public office. Therefore, Americans must pay more attention and engage in the political process to hold these officials accountable and remove them from office, regardless of how difficult this might be or how long it may take when they fail to represent the will of the people who elected them.

Americans are innovators. When faced with what seem like unsolvable problems, history illustrates that Americans will find a way forward. My parents growing up in the Jim Crow South governed by public office holders from the Democrat Party were influenced by the Civil Rights movement. This environment shaped their ideas on how to conduct their lives and raise their children. They taught me how to live freely despite obstacles that might be placed in my way.

Liberty starts in a person's mind. If you do not think you are free, then you are not. The segregated south was no match for my parents and my uncle's dreams. They each had a vision of a better life that continually motivated them to keep moving forward. They taught me how to grasp and hang on to the American value of liberty, despite the efforts of those who would attempt to deny me that unalienable right.

## **INSIGHTS ON GLOBAL LIBERTY**

Traveling to, and living in, various places around the world at a young age gave me a broad perspective on how countries are governed. Liberty is not a common trait present in many counties around the world. Before I entered college at the United States Air Force Academy at the age of seventeen, I visited the following countries or island land masses: Benin, Cameroon, Denmark, France, Hong Kong, Iran, Italy, Japan, Malaysia, the Netherlands, Okinawa, Penang, the Philippines, Singapore, Spain, Switzerland, Taiwan, the United Kingdom, and Vietnam. I lived in Nigeria for three years and in Thailand for six and a half years.

Many things I witnessed or heard about during that time in my life I would not fully understand until I was much older. A period of political unrest in Indonesia prevented the rest of our family from joining my father in 1959, when he worked there on a grant administered through Tuskegee Institute located in Tuskegee, Alabama. He was hired to help the government of Indonesia transition some of their cottage industries into businesses through developing their vocational education system.

I experienced a coup firsthand while living in Nigeria. On October 1, 1960, Nigeria became a sovereign nation with Abubakar Tafawa Balewa serving as the country's first federal prime minster.[68] Then, however, "... [A]*fter the collapse of order in the west* [of Nigeria] *following the fraudulent election of October 1965, a group of army officers attempted to overthrow the federal government, and Balewa and two of the regional premiers were murdered.*"[69]

Another example is connected to the time I attended school in Bangkok from 1967 through 1973, which overlapped Mao Zedong's reign of terror in Communist China. A classmate who sat next to me in Math Analysis Class during my junior year of high school was a young man from mainland or Red China. At times we had interesting discussions about his country of birth. As part of the usual graduation traditions, he wrote a note in Mandarin in my yearbook, but many years passed before I found someone who could translate the note for me. His note in the year book could be summarized as, "Thanks for your friendship and always remember the good times we had together."

Though we came from two very different cultures, the time we spent in high school together, and particularly that so regular-sounding note, showed me how he and I had more in common than differences. We were simply two adolescents growing up in yet another culture other than our own. Unfortunately, we did not keep in touch, nor did we reconnect later in life. Since the culture in China does not nurture liberty, I wonder even today how his carefree attitude and cheerful outlook on life served him after he returned to his homeland.

## LIBERTY AROUND THE GLOBE

Since Thailand was so close to China and also Hong Kong (which I visited several times), I gained some insight into this vast country and the hardship its people experienced under communist rule during the Cultural Revolution.[70] Mao rallied the youth, called the Red Guard, to carry out his plan to secure power, and it is estimated that these violent youth persecuted 36 million people in rural China and killed between 750,000 to 1.5 million people.[71]

The Revolution was "a chaotic time of uncertainty when education abruptly shut down and family and local ties were severed," and today the Chinese refer to this as the lost decade from 1966 to 1976 and are very reluctant to talk about it.[72] Thailand also bordered Laos which was affected by the Vietnam War.

While I lived in Thailand, my father worked and spent most of his time in Vietnam. He would come to Bangkok to visit once a month for a week. In early January of 1968, the U.S. Agency for International Development, or USAID, my father's employer, determined that things were quiet enough for families to visit Vietnam. Thus, I was able to visit my father in Bien Hoa near a major U.S. Air Base located in the south-central part of the country.

I thoroughly enjoyed the trip, and took my first helicopter ride in a UH-1 Huey. My mother and I spent a week in Bien Hoa. On January 21, 1968, a week after we returned to Thailand, a diversionary attack against an American base at Khe Sanh was conducted before the start of the Tet Offensive on January 30, 1968, by the commanding general of the North Vietnamese Army, General Vo Nguyen Giap.[73]

During the Tet Offensive over 100 cities were attacked, which completely surprised the Americans and the South Vietnamese. Needless to say, families were no longer allowed to visit Vietnam after that time.

Thailand also bordered Cambodia where, after I left Thailand from 1975 to 1979, Pol Pot of the Communist Khmer Rouge regime committed genocide by murdering three million people, or one quarter of the population.[74] From China to Vietnam to Cambodia, I came to understand that the relative stability in the United States resulting from the excellent principles rooted in our Constitution and the rule of law was not common in other counties.

In many countries a change of leadership, especially in developing nations, might involve conflicts resulting in fighting and sometimes the death of opposition or outgoing leaders, and those thrown out of office would, at minimum, end up in prison.

Though the U.S. has experienced turbulent times in the recent past, such as in 1968 when Martian Luther King, Jr., and Robert F. Kennedy were assassinated, and the country was in turmoil riddled with racial unrest, the leadership of the country remained firmly in place. This stability assured that liberty was maintained for the citizens. Other countries have not fared so well when they experienced such internal strife.

## **LIBERTY AS A STATE OF MIND**

A different way of looking at liberty is being careful to think about the influences that affect what a person will do. You will act in the way you think. You control what is in your mind, no one else.

I received encouragement from my mother one day while I was in the middle of high school, and I chose an activity that I wanted to do but my friends were not interested in doing. High school boys clump together. I had my close friends that I enjoyed being around. We did many activities together and solved all the world's problems when we talked into the wee hours of the morning. Since I was interested in science, and in particular the manned space program, I would always take the opportunity to enjoy anything related to this subject. I liked reading Science Fiction books written by some of my favorite authors like Ray Bradbury who wrote, *The Martian Chronicles*, and especially *2001: A Space Odyssey*, written by Arthur C. Clark, and Isaac Asimov's, book, *I, Robot*. When famous film producer Stanley Kubrick worked with Clark and produced the movie, *2001 A Space Odyssey*, in 1968 I had to see it right away when it came to the movie theater.

On the afternoon when I'd planned to go see this movie, my friends were in my room as they usually were on Saturday. After a few hours they left. When my mom saw me emerge from the room by myself, she asked me what had happened because usually all of us would leave together. I let her know that I wanted to see the movie, *2001: A Space Odyssey*, and that the others didn't want to spend their money or take the time to go to this movie. So, I decided to go by myself.

My mother congratulated me on doing something that was important to me and not being swayed by the group. At the time, I didn't think much of her comment although I appreciated the encouragement. Now that I've raised four children and understand the ins-and-outs of how young people, especially teenagers, influence each other, I thoroughly understand what my mother was talking about way back then when I was in high school.

I had the liberty to exercise my personal freedom because I was taught by my parents to do so. I didn't let the crowd take away from me what I wanted to do. I determined what I thought and decided how I would act; I didn't let someone or some group decide for me.

## AN ESSENTIAL LIBERTY LESSON FOR ME

My mother looked for a better path leading to a future with opportunities by seeking more education. This enabled her to enter the nursing profession when she graduated from Hampton Institute. The nursing profession gave her more personal freedom because it enabled her to have more job opportunities and more control over how she used her time.

Mom left North Carolina to seek work in New Jersey after attending high school in North Carolina. She was hired as a domestic helper by a family. My sister relayed a story that after a time of working for them, the woman of the house who had hired her remarked, "Dorothy, I'm going to make a good domestic worker out of you." "Domestic worker," of course, was not the goal that my mother had in mind for her future because working in this capacity would limit how she would be able to spend her time and what goals she could pursue.

Fortunately, she was soon hired by another family, the Mountcastles, who saw her differently and recognized her potential. With their help, she eventually reached her goal of becoming a nurse which gave her much more liberty than she would have had as a domestic helper.

As I explained in Chapter 1, my Uncle Gordon had a difficult time obtaining a job as an electrical engineer, the profession that he was educated to enter. It took him fourteen years before this became a reality. He was persistent. In the end he reached his goal and served the General Electric Company (G.E.) well as an Electrical Engineer. Just as in my mother's instance, my Uncle Gordon believed with America's value of liberty backing him up, he could get to where he intended to be, and he did.

My mother and uncle taught me the valuable lesson that if you dream about reaching a goal, you should pursue that goal. America is a country where liberty includes pursuing your dreams. Do not give up. Keep striving.

I dreamed of being a pilot. I am convinced that I was born with jet fuel in my veins, despite what the doctors might say. However, some in the world around me did not necessarily think that me becoming a pilot would really happen. My parents were very surprised when I succeeded. My sister, who is four years older than me, wasn't surprised at all because she always said that I drew pictures of airplanes before I learned how to write my ABCs.

## I Dreamed and Became a Pilot

Though my path to aviation began when I was born, I recall that I consciously started thinking about becoming a pilot when I had my first commercial airplane ride when I was seven years old. In 1963, my father was hired by the United Nations (U.N.), which caused our family to travel from Philadelphia to Lagos, Nigeria. On the first day of our travels, I flew in a propeller airplane from Philadelphia to New York City, and then in a jet from New York City to London, England. It was exciting. However, a significant event occurred a few days later when I was aboard a KLM, Royal Dutch Airline, Boeing 707 out of London, while flying into Amsterdam, a city located in the Netherlands, or Holland.

Since this was in the day prior to hijackings there was no door on the cockpit. A curtain that was rarely closed to cover the doorway hung from the top of the door frame and was tied back and fastened to one side of the cockpit doorway. The curtain was open during much of the flight. The captain, noticing me standing by the doorway, invited me into the cockpit. He even let me sit on his lap and look at all the controls. I remember that everything was very interesting, especially all the instruments. However, when I looked out of the windshield and saw a very deep blue sky, filled with white puffy clouds, as we made a descending turn to a lower altitude, I saw the very colorful fields of tulips in bloom on the ground in Amsterdam.

This beautiful picture completely captured my full attention. Something clicked in my mind, and I said to myself, "I can do this." That was the moment. I knew then that I was going to become a pilot.

About two years later I had an opportunity to meet Astronaut John Glenn when he visited Lagos as he traveled around the world following his February 20, 1962, historic space flight on the Mercury-Atlas 6 mission aboard the spacecraft he named Friendship 7. On that mission, he became the first American to orbit the earth, circling the world three times.[75] I was impressed and knew that aviation was where I needed to be. I now also wanted to become a Test Pilot and perhaps an Astronaut. It was 1963 and I was seven years old.

Years later, when I attended the United States Air Force Academy, I reaffirmed my goal to become a Test Pilot. In 2003 I lived in Dayton, Ohio, the birthplace of aviation which held a 100-year celebration of the 1903 invention of flight by Wilbur and Orville Wright. At this celebration I had the privilege of meeting Senator Glenn again and reminded him of our first meeting decades earlier and thanked him for motivating me to become a Test Pilot as he had been.

He and I had a nice talk concerning the B-2 when he learned that I had flown that airplane. He also had the opportunity to fly the B-2 with John Belanger, who served as his instructor pilot during the flight. John and I were Second Lieutenants together at Carswell Air Force base where the Air Force first assigned us to fly the B-52D.

I continued the pathway to reach my goal of becoming a pilot. I learned that many engineers became pilots, so I focused on Math and Science in high school. I also discovered that the Air Force Academy was the only college during this time that offered Astronautical Engineering as an undergraduate degree. In addition, I knew that going there would give me an excellent chance to become a pilot.

Now there was just one problem that never really bothered me but began to bother some other people. Namely, I wear glasses. I've always worn glasses. Fortunately, my vision was 20/25 in my left eye and 20/30 in my right eye without my glasses, and even more fortunately, my glasses corrected my vision to 20/20 in both eyes. My overall vision wasn't that bad.

I found out that the Air Force at this time would grant flying waivers for pilots if they had vision up to 20/50 correctable to 20/20, so I knew then I had a chance, but many others didn't see it that way.

I remember walking into the office of the Air Force Attaché at the American Embassy in Bangkok, Thailand during my junior year of high school asking how I should go about applying to the Air Force Academy. The Attaché advises the American Ambassador, who is the senior U.S. representative in a foreign country. He took one look at my glasses and said that I would never be accepted. My eighth-grade science teacher laughed at me in class one day when she asked everyone what they wanted to be when they grew up, and when it was my turn, I said I wanted to be a pilot. I even had one of my childhood friends who lived on my street back in Philadelphia remark that I would never go to the Air Force Academy because "they didn't let Black people in there."

There were many who told me what I couldn't do. However, there were many more who cheered me on and did all they could to help me reach my goal. Many were teachers, some of whom wrote letters of recommendation for me to enter the Academy. There were pilots who also encouraged me, and there were family members who were on my side. Chapter 2 provides a more detailed account of my pilot journey. My dream became reality, and I had an abundance of rousing adventures as a result.

> I became a pilot. I did not let anyone deter me from my goal. Because I'm an American, I had the liberty to dream and reach for my goal. The country of my birth gave me that opportunity. My parents and my uncle taught me to never give up through the example of their lives and with their encouraging words. I trusted them and listened to them. I had the liberty to become the successful person I dreamed I'd be.

# 6

## FAITH

*"Our Constitution was made only for a moral and religious people. It is wholly inadequate to the Government of any other."*
—**John Adams,** 2nd *U.S. President, October 11, 1798*[76]

*"Now faith is the assurance of things hoped for, the conviction of things not seen."*
—**Hebrews 11:1 ESV**

Faith is a core American value. It guided our founding fathers as they wrestled with forming this county. Many of them had very different views regarding how they worshiped, but they came together and agreed that they were accountable to God for their actions and sought His guidance in their very solemn undertaking.[77] The founding fathers reached that end when the Constitution of the United States was ratified by all thirteen colonies.[78]

Faith was evident in my family, passed from my grandparents on my father's side to him and his brothers and sisters, to me, and from my mother's side, from her grandmother to her to me. Going to church was important. The importance of faith was instilled in me and helped me to develop successfully in life. It guided my sense of being, why I was on the earth, showed me how to treat others, and what I should expect from the world we live in.

## BUILDING BLOCKS OF MY FAITH—CHURCH

My earliest memories of going to church centered around the First Presbyterian Church located on Germantown Avenue in Philadelphia, Pennsylvania, where my parents took our family to worship. The church building looked grand and distinctive. Inside there were high ceilings with light pouring through the stained-glass windows. This environment gave a feeling of being in the presence of something different and out of the ordinary. Out of respect for others, people were silent or spoke softly when in the sanctuary. I remember going to this church listening to sermons and I remember Sunday school when I was about nine years old.

In Thailand my family attended the International Church on Soi or Street 19. The street was also called Soi Wattana. The building was owned by the Church of Christ, not the American denomination of the Church of Christ, but an organization formed in Thailand. The church was led by the Reverend Erwin Ruklik, a Presbyterian minister. He greatly influenced me to become a Christian as he presented the gospel in his sermons with most of the Sunday school teachers supporting this message when they taught us. But it was Reverend Ruklik who spent individual time helping me look into my faith and pursue spiritual growth.

When I was about eleven, I became a Christian, meaning that I personally put my trust in Jesus Christ as my Lord and Savior. However, one moment I am not proud of occurred one Sunday when I was in high school; I decided to give my mother grief, and I intentionally did not get dressed in time to ride with her when she drove the family car to the church service. She paused for a moment, looked at me, did not say a word and left for church without me. I was surprised by the lack of scolding from her, which I expected. Neither did she talk to me about the incident when she returned.

Reflecting back, I have to admit I was very high-spirited and would not want any parent to have had to deal with me when I was in my teens. My dad, working in Vietnam three weeks out of every month, left my mom to be both mom and dad most of the time—a very difficult task. Mom kept a tight rein on me, which is probably why I turned out as well as I did.

In any case, after this incident, it seemed like going to church was something I wanted to do and not something I felt like I had to do. There was never a time after this incident while growing up that I chose not to attend the church service.

Reverend Ruklik also helped me earn the Boy Scouts of America God and Country Award. While working on the God and Country Award, Reverend Ruklik sent me to meet with a missionary who was born in the country of Burma, now called Myanmar, that is on the western border of Thailand. I was fascinated listening to his experiences of how he became a Christian and how he became a Christian missionary.

He was also a minister, and I was captivated by the stories of serving as a missionary in his home country of Burma. They were amazing! Coups that led to military rule had made his work too dangerous to continue, so he'd moved to Thailand. He hoped his stay there would be temporary.

The Church was a major part of my life when I was in Thailand, especially as I moved into high school. The International Church had a very active youth group that I participated in. We had wonderful youth leaders, who took us on youth retreats and guided us to seriously think about our faith in God and the impact it had on the way we lived.

Throughout my early childhood, I regularly attended a Messiah[79] performance during the Christmas season. I also very much enjoyed singing in the choir during the annual Messiah concerts conducted at Christmastime in Bangkok, Thailand. Though there was no snow on the ground because Thailand is a tropical country, the concert reminded me of Christmas celebrations in Philadelphia, Pennsylvania, which I considered my hometown.

Two of the talented soloists who participated in this event in Bangkok that I especially remember were Mrs. Lamb, a soprano who also was a teacher at the International School of Bangkok (ISB), and Reverend

Gregory, who had a deep rich bass voice. His children were my friends, and Reverend Gregory served as a Christian missionary in Thailand.

At the Air Force Academy every year, we sang the Messiah by joining with choirs from downtown Colorado Springs or Denver because, until my senior year the Air Force Academy was an all-male institution, so we did not have the female voices necessary to perform this music. We performed the Messiah in the Air Force Academy chapel which was beautiful and awe inspiring.

I spent quite a bit of time in the chapel because I was a member of the Protestant choir and the Cadet Chorale. We performed many times in the chapel in addition to singing during weekly church services. During the years that I have not had the opportunity to do this, it seemed like something was missing at Christmas.

A unique and memorable Messiah performance I witnessed featured a choir and a full orchestra and also included classical ballet dancers on the stage. This performance took place when I was stationed at the Pentagon in Washington, D.C.

Having the opportunity to sing sacred Christian music regularly helped strengthen my faith.

## DIGGING IN

When I attended pilot training, going to the Air Force Chapel was very important. It was an extension of going to the chapel at the academy, and the Air Force Chapel became a central place of worship for me once I entered the Air Force. During pilot training I was 21 years old and that was when, for the first time, I started teaching Sunday school. If you want to learn something well, teach sixth graders, because they will ask questions about anything related or not related to the subject. At this time in my life I was young, and teaching biblical truths became an important activity in my spiritual development.

During my time at the Air Force Academy, I had visited a Bible study run by the Officers' Christian Fellowship. Much later in my Air Force career this organization would become very important. The Officers' Christian Fellowship, or OCF, began in 1943 and grew out of a British organization, the Officers' Christian Union, started in 1919 by British military men.[80] The organization can reach out to military personnel anywhere that military personnel may be, on the battlefield, on ships, or on military bases. OCF ministers to, or takes care of, the needs of military members in situations where it would not necessarily seem likely that there would be spiritual support. OCF is a great help to military chaplains who do excellent work all over the military.

I also participated in activities organized by the Navigators at the Air Force Academy. The Navigators hosted Bible studies that some of my classmates and I attended during pilot training. The Navigators are an international Christian organization, with a headquarters in Colorado Springs, Colorado. The Navigators was started by Dawson Trotman, a California lumberyard[81] worker, who emphasized memorizing Bible verses and growing in Christlikeness through accountability to other likeminded Christians, or what is also called Discipleship, referring to Jesus teaching His disciples.[82]

Becoming an Air Force pilot requires a disciplined focus. Student pilots must learn to follow all of the procedures necessary to fly aircraft according to Air Force regulations. The Navigators had a great effect on my spiritual development, as I was learning how to become a pilot and just starting on the beginning of my Air Force career.

The organization helped me discipline myself to methodically study the Bible for the purpose of understanding what God requires of His followers in Scripture passages and how to apply them in life. They taught this disciplined approach in a systematic way and in structured Bible studies that helped individuals learn and retain the information, and their disciplined approach to developing spiritually was similar to that required by the Air Force to become a pilot.

After I moved on from Williams Air Force Base, Arizona, to Carswell Air Force Base in Fort Worth, Texas, my first assignment, I again looked up the Navigator group and became part of it. I also joined an Officers' Christian Fellowship Bible study group. The Carswell Air Force Base chapel was the main place I attended church while I was assigned there, although I did occasionally visit other churches in Fort Worth.

At Carswell, I volunteered to help with the Base youth and was asked to be the Assistant Director of the youth group. The Director,

Patrick Stewart, a Baptist Minister, became a close friend while he was going through seminary at Southwestern Seminary in Fort Worth, Texas, at that time. When his course load became too heavy, I took over for him as Youth Group Director, which I enjoyed. I also taught high school Sunday School.

One of the important aspects of my relationship with Pat is that he really challenged me with thinking through my spiritual beliefs. He introduced me to a few authors who eventually became some of my favorite authors, especially Francis Schaeffer, a Presbyterian minister. Since Dr. Schaeffer and I are both from Pennsylvania, I especially appreciated his examples taken from our common area of the United States. They were readily understandable for me.

Dr. Schaeffer was also brilliant and probably will be considered one of the greatest philosophers and theologians of the 20th century. I was very impressed reading some of his books such as *Death in The City*, and *The God Who Is There*, and particularly, *Escape From Reason*. But I'd say the book that impacted me most was, *Whatever Happened to The Human Race*, which he wrote with C. Everett Koop, MD, who was U.S. Surgeon General at the time. This book discussed euthanasia (killing of the old or seriously ill), infanticide (killing infants) and abortion (killing babies). When I read the book, I could not believe that what he thought would happen in the future in our society would come true. Sadly, today it is happening.

I also absorbed books written by John R.W. Stott and J.C. Ryle. If Bishop Ryle's book, *Thoughts for Young Men*, were widely read today, I think it would have a positive impact on the youth of our society. Additionally, Arthur Pink's book, *The Sovereignty of God*, is an excellent read. All these suggestions were in addition to studying the Bible with purpose.

I decided at that point in my life to read the Bible regularly instead of occasionally. Being stationed at Carswell Air Force Base and having the opportunity to get to know Pat Stewart was very important because Pat helped me understand my spiritual Christian viewpoint clearly. That viewpoint has guided me through the rest of my life.

After Carswell Air Force Base, I was assigned to Osan Air Base, in the Republic of Korea where there was a tight knit group of Christians.

During my time there I enjoyed getting to know several Christians, especially Air Force Major General Fred A. Haeffner, the Commander of the 314th Air Division with its headquarters located at Osan Air Base. He oversaw the American air forces in Korea. Major General Haeffner hosted a weekly Bible study in his house at six o'clock in the morning. A core group of people amassed and prayed for each other, and especially for our leaders.

The United States never really ceased war with North Korea. An armistice was signed on July 27, 1953, because the Korean war reached a stalemate.[83] So at any time, things could erupt in a hot conflict between North and South Korea. War almost did erupt on October 9, 1983, when South Korea's President, Chun Doo-hwan was visiting Burma and the North Koreans attempted to blow up his car.[84] Because the president's car arrived later than scheduled, the explosion missed him. The South Koreans were sure that the North Koreans were behind this incident, so they responded by preparing to go to war with the North.

While stationed in Korea, the unofficial feeling the rank-and-file U.S. military members held was that the American forces in Korea were not there to protect South Korea from North Korea. They were there to restrain South Korea from going north. The Koreans do not like being divided and strongly desire to be reunited because they believe Koreans are one people and they are a very proud people. However, since they are governed by two completely different systems of government, one Democratic and the other Socialist, resolving their differences and uniting has not been possible.

When the attempted assassination of the South Korean President brought them to the brink of war, Major General Haeffner attended some of the meetings with South Korean military leaders where they discussed war. He was a voice of reason by helping them think through the tense situation.

The Korean leaders eventually realized responding by going to war with the North was not a good solution. One reason they decided against war was that Seoul, the capital of South Korea, was chosen to host the 1988 Olympic Games. If the two countries had gone to war the games would not have been held there. So, a U.S. military officer who professed Christianity helped to keep the world from entering another embroiled conflict on the Korean peninsula. In this instance, a man of faith helped diffuse a tense international situation.

I thanked God then, and I thank God now for his guidance through challenging situations.

While stationed in Korea, I returned to the United States briefly to marry my wife, Donna, and immediately brought her back to Korea with me. Since I'd dated her for four years, I decided it was time.... she'd been very patient! We spent our first wonderful year of marriage in Korea.

A major reason I thought Donna and I were a great match was her Christian faith and that we were each at the same point in the development of our Christian life when we met. This gave us a common ground on which to base our marriage and begin our life together. It is a blessing for us to travel through life going in the same direction. We were married in the beautiful Air Force Academy chapel June 10, 1983, and then traveled to Korea.

After Korea, the Air Force assigned me to Plattsburgh Air Force Base located on scenic Lake Champlain in upstate New York. I became more actively involved in the Officers' Christian Fellowship there. Because Officers' Christian Fellowship did not have a group at Plattsburgh Air Force Base, the organization asked me to start one, and I agreed.

That decision blessed Donna and me with meeting two of our eventually dearest friends, Ward and his wife Bobbie Graham. The Officers' Christian Fellowship sent Ward to help start the group at Plattsburgh Air Force Base, and he had a small private airplane that he used to fly he and his wife from White Sulfur Springs, Pennsylvania, to where we were in upstate New York.

Ward was a retired Air Force Lieutenant Colonel and an outstanding U-2 pilot. The U-2 is a single engine reconnaissance airplane that flies at high altitude and gathers intelligence information. It flies so high that the pilot must wear a pressure suit. This suit looks very much like what astronauts wear in space.

Ward experienced some very dangerous emergencies while flying the U-2. On one of these occasions, he had to dead stick the U-2, or fly it without the help of the engine, because it was shut down and as a result was forced to land on the desert floor.

Ward and I were kindred spirits, sharing the love of piloting airplanes. Another great addition to the OCF team was Glenn Rogers, one of the Plattsburgh Air Force Base Chaplains.

In the recent past Glenn lived in Philadelphia, Pennsylvania, so he and I also shared a common culture. Glenn was a Bible Presbyterian pastor and an outstanding preacher. We developed a very close relationship. Glenn was at Plattsburgh for the birth of our first child and prayed over him. Later, he was stationed at Edwards Air Force Base and baptized that same child. My wife and I considered this a tremendous blessing.

Glenn Rogers, like Pat Stewart, was also very important in helping me develop spiritually. During my last years in the Air Force, Glenn became the chaplain for the B-2 Test Squadron I commanded at Edwards Air Force Base, California. When I served as the squadron commander, it was encouraging having my good friend Glenn by my side to offer advice.

I remained part of the Officers' Christian Fellowship throughout my Air Force career, and for many years afterwards. I even served on the organization's governing council. It was an honor to be part of the group that planned for and guided the direction of this wonderful organization.

While serving on the council, I met many outstanding Christian military officers. The Officers' Christian Fellowship is a very important organization to the spiritual well-being of military members of our society.

Faith is a central part in the lives of my wife and me. We raised our children in a Christian home environment. It was our privilege to have the opportunity to explain spiritual principles to them, and to see them grow and develop in their knowledge of the Lord, as we helped them learn how to read their Bibles and encouraged them to participate in organizations that helped support that growth. We attended church as a family, which was very central in our lives, wherever we lived.

In many of these places, the children were able to take part in a Christian organization called AWANA, which stands for Approved

Workmen Are Not Ashamed, a paraphrase of the Bible verse 2 Timothy 2:15. This organization inside churches teaches the children to memorize Bible verses, which is the Word of God, and helps to transform lives to do His will.

When a person says Bible verses, reads and memorizes them, the words in the Bible actually have an effect on a person's life more noticeably than the normal written words by man because men's words are men's words, but the Bible is the Word of God.

It is amazing to see how faith changes the way people live their lives. One of my friends, Reggie[85], who I knew at the Air Force Academy, was hard on others and had a rough personality.

He generally had a hard expression on his face when he looked at you, the kind of expression common to those who lived in the inner city of large urban areas to warn others not to mess with you. And if he spoke, he would first strike a pose where he leaned toward you expanding his chest to make himself look bigger to assert himself in an intimidating manner. His voice was loud, harsh, and demanding. The colloquial expression is that he would, "get in your face." Reggie sounded and behaved in the way many have come to expect from people who live in "The Big Apple," as New York City is often referred to.

Yet many years later, when I saw him after we both retired from the Air Force and were members of the same church, he behaved very differently. He was calm and down to earth. No longer was every conversation a possible confrontation. He was a good father and solid family man. He credited his transformation to his faith by becoming a Christian and changing his priorities to serve Jesus Christ.

Another remarkable experience I had in terms of experiencing a changed life first-hand was my friend, Paul Higgins. Paul was one of the cadets I knew at the Air Force Academy. We both majored in Astronautical Engineering or Astro.

Near the end of our senior year, the Astro Department divided the seniors into two competing companies and gave us a design project. Paul was the CEO of one of the companies. Paul was the kind of guy that you wanted beside you in a knife fight. He was very loyal and fiercely defended his friends.

My close friend in pilot training, John Graper, who I shared a kitchen with, and I were also prayer partners. We often prayed specifically for other friends who were members of our pilot training class to become Christians.

One day after we prayed for our mutual friend Paul Higgins, I asked John if he really thought that Paul would ever become a Christian. John quietly reminded me that nothing is impossible for God to do.

Many years after graduating from pilot training, I was in Korea taking part in a major military exercise called Team Spirit. In the middle of one night during the exercise I was on duty with some pilots who were stationed at Davis-Monthan Air Force Base located in Tucson, Arizona. I asked them if they ever ran into a guy by the name of Paul Higgins, who was a friend of mine who was stationed at their Base.

One of the guys nodded and said, "Yes." He went on, "You know, Paul was a great guy. I really enjoyed being around him. He'd go out drinking with us, and we'd have a lot of fun. Then one day, he brought a Bible into the squadron and started hanging around with this Christian girl. After that he just wasn't one of the guys anymore. He totally changed!"

My jaw dropped when I heard this story. It was my privilege at our class of 1977 40th reunion at the Air Force Academy to relay the Korea story to Paul, and it made him laugh. I had not seen him since we were cadets 40 years before. So, we talked about living as Christians.

Even before the reunion I'd connected with Paul on Facebook, so we'd exchanged notes earlier about him becoming a Christian. Discussing this topic looking at each other face-to-face, I had the privilege of telling him how John Graper and I prayed for him many years ago during pilot training to become a Christian.

Paul had become a powerful Christian man. It was great to see him at our 40th class reunion and to have the pleasure of meeting his wife. Paul is humble and church is very important to him. He has a ministry where he drives around and helps the elderly who are not very mobile to be able to attend church.

Recognizing how the Spirit of God moving through the Word of God can affect people is exciting to me. In my life and travels, I've had many opportunities to see the value of faith, and for this I am grateful.

# FAITH STORIES
## KAZAKHSTAN: THE WAITRESS ENCOUNTER

On a FedEx trip in December of 2003, I flew from Hong Kong to Almaty, Kazakhstan. I looked forward to flying there because it was a Soviet Satellite Republic and a place where I would have the opportunity to speak Russian, the language I'd studied at the Air Force Academy. It is now a sovereign nation and part of the Commonwealth of Independent States.[86] The city is in southeastern Kazakhstan, in a valley at the base of the Trans-Ili Alatau mountains, where the landscape is green hills, lakes, and wide pastures.

Since I'd only taken one year of Russian, I was nowhere even close to being able to carry on a conversation with my very limited vocabulary. But I used the few words and phrases I knew, and since the Kazakh's responded to me with broad smiles and muffled laughter, I'm sure my broken Russian humored them. As an example, early one morning when going for a swim in the hotel pool, I surprised the attendant when I asked her for a towel. She exclaimed in English, "You speak clean Russian. I can understand you!" before handing me my towel.

The flight to Almaty had required three pilots because of distance covered. The Captain was Joe Osborne, the First Officer was Mike Healy, and I was the relief First Officer. We were in the air for about fourteen hours. Once we landed, we had a three-day break in our flying schedule before we would fly to our next destination.

After arriving at the hotel, we decided to eat dinner at a Kazakh restaurant. Since I was the broken-Russian speaker, the other two elected me to go down to the hotel lobby and ask the concierge for help. When I let her know our plan, the concierge wrote on a piece of paper in Russian the name and address of a restaurant she recommended. She then told me to give this paper to the taxi driver who would meet us at 6 P.M. that evening in the hotel lobby.

It was wintertime in Almaty and there was quite a bit of snow on the ground. When the three of us met in the lobby and looked toward the hotel entrance, we noticed a man walking toward us. The bellman at the entrance told us that this was our taxi driver.

Ivan, our driver, was wearing sunglasses though it was dark outside, and we noticed a long scar on the side of his face stretching from his sideburn to the bottom of his jaw. The three of us looked at each other for a moment and then back at Ivan. Ivan saw that we were a little hesitant, so he motioned us to come with him.

Once outside the hotel, we followed Ivan and got into a black car that looked like it was built in the 1950s. After riding for about fifteen minutes, we noticed the lights of the city had faded into the deepening night. Everything was dark including the inside of the car. We wondered if we were ever going to be seen again. Was our silent, mysterious driver abducting us?

After another ten to fifteen more minutes, we stopped in front of a gate, probably about eight to 10 feet tall, with a small door cut out in it. The cutout door was open. Ivan motioned for us to get out of the car. We really did not want to, but at that moment we saw there was a man standing in the open doorway motioning with his hand for us to come with him, so we followed the gentleman through the doorway.

Once past the doorway in the gate, we found ourselves walking through a fenced courtyard filled with tables and chairs. Because it was winter, it seemed normal that the courtyard would have no people in it. Then, rounding a corner, we saw a well-lit building and welcomed the warm air that surrounded us as we went inside. We were in a very nice restaurant.

The man led us to a table and we sat down. Our waitress, Kathy, was very friendly and spoke perfect English. She was a paradox. If you weren't looking at her while she spoke, you would think you were talking with someone from New York; her accent was perfect! Looking at her, however, you would know she was from Asia, in hair style, clothing, and body gestures, very much like the people I saw walking along the streets of Almaty. She guided us through many courses of food and drink, as we thoroughly enjoyed ourselves throughout the evening.

The restaurant featured belly dancers wearing very colorful traditional dress. I couldn't have had a more unique way of celebrating my 48th birthday. Yes this evening was a particularly special occasion for me. Moments after Kathy found this out, one of the belly dancers came over to the table and pulled me onto the dance floor where I proceeded to make a fool of myself! It was all very festive.

Ultimately, we asked Kathy how she learned to speak English so well. She responded, "Well, my family is from North Korea. When I was very young, American missionaries in North Korea who came to live in my village taught me English.

We were dumbfounded and said, "They taught you well!" Then we asked how did she come to live in Kazakhstan? She told us her family walked out of North Korea and traveled on a long journey and eventually settled in Uzbekistan.

The three of us discussed this amazing story for about ten or fifteen more minutes. Then we asked her, "If your family traveled from North Korea to Uzbekistan, how is it you are working in a Kazakh restaurant?"

Kathy responded, "Oh, this isn't a Kazakh restaurant, this is an Uzbek restaurant." Uzbekistan is another former Soviet satellite state, located just southeast of Kazakhstan. Kathy later talked to our taxi driver and learned that he hadn't taken us to the restaurant written on the paper we'd given him. Ivan's brother-in-law owned the restaurant we were in, so he'd driven us there.

We all chuckled when we realized it really didn't matter where we wanted to go, we were going where the driver wanted us to go instead. So maybe we were abducted.... regardless, we had a great meal!

I fondly remember that night of camaraderie, but I also took note then and find inspiring that our waitress was fluent in English due to the dedication of American missionaries who, despite grave personal risk, were eager to live among people in another country to spread the gospel of Jesus Christ. They taught Kathy when she was a young child growing up in North Korea.

Her family escaped on foot and she ended up speaking in perfect New York English to the three of us that night. Kathy illustrates the positive influence of those of faith on other nations around the world. God is good.

## The Wycliffe Translator

Driving the three hours between Subic Bay to Manila in the Philippines was not wise because thieves sometimes attacked unsuspecting travelers. Not only would they steal from you but meeting these characters could put your life in danger.

Since the drive was long and unsafe, FedEx provided a small twin-engine airplane, known as the Twin Otter, to shuttle people between the two cities. The main purpose of the shuttle was to move pilots from Subic Bay to Manila International Airport, so that they could fly on a passenger airline on what is called a deadhead trip. These trips were scheduled to make sure the pilot was in the city where the next FedEx flight he was scheduled to fly would depart from early enough to be ready to operate that flight.

Usually there were empty seats on the Twin Otter because only a few pilots would be scheduled to deadhead on any given day. Sometimes no FedEx pilots were scheduled for this purpose. Family members were allowed to fly on the Twin Otter to Manila if there were empty seats available. So I would take my oldest son to Manila, homeschool him in the morning, and then take him to his weekly violin lesson. We would also attend an American Boy Scout meeting in the evening.

After the meeting, we would stay overnight and the next day return to Subic Bay. Sometimes when we stayed overnight, we had the opportunity to stay in the Wycliffe Bible Translators hostel where the translators who lived and worked very far from Manila would stay. Some of the translators worked in remote islands in the Philippines, but many of them worked in various remote areas of Indonesia.

The work of the Wycliffe translators[87] in Indonesia was especially interesting because it is the most populous Muslim country on the face of the earth. The Wycliffe Bible Translators is a Christian organization started in 1942 that is committed to translating the Bible, the Word of God, into the local language. The Indonesian government appreciates their work with the indigenous people in various tribal areas.

The Wycliffe Bible Translators work for years to learn the language of the people and then to complete the translation of the Bible. After Gutenberg's invention of the printing press, in the history of the

Protestant Reformation, one of the most important achievements that increased the spread of Christianity was having the Bible written in the language the people could read.

Wycliffe's mission continues today as Bible translators travel around the world to very isolated people groups to make sure that they have the Word of God in their own language so that they can read and understand it. This work is extremely important because the Word of God transforms lives. So far the Wycliffe Bible Translators have translated the Bible into around 1,600 languages.

One day, my son and I were at the Wycliffe Bible Translator's hostel in Manila before traveling back to the airport to board the Twin Otter and return to Subic Bay. We were eating breakfast with a gentleman who was working in Indonesia. I asked him about his work. He shared a very interesting story with us that took place in a remote place in Indonesia where he worked translating the local language.

He was at the end of his time there, and had finished translating the Bible and was preparing to return to the United States. He told us that one day a government official came to visit the tribe by helicopter. When the helicopter landed, the tribal chief ran up to the official wildly waving a machete in the face of the official and yelling.

The Chief then pointed the machete at the translator, and said to the official, "If you had come here, years ago, I would have killed you and eaten you because we were cannibals. But because of this man who came and showed us the Word of God, we are no longer cannibals. We now believe that people are made in the image of God, and we shouldn't be killing them to eat as food. We wouldn't have known this truth if this man had not come here. I just want you to know that this man helped us change the way we've lived for generations."

This kind of change in understanding is profound. Consider the fact that the translators traveled to work with this tribe in a remote part of Indonesia where the people were cannibals! Through a translator's dedication and calling to learn the language of the people and translate the Word of God into that language, and then teach the people the Word of God, different groups of isolated people completely change their lifestyle and become people of faith.

This is faith being put to the test.

## **MIKE AND EVE BROOKS**

I met Mike and Eve Brooks while I was training to become an Air Force pilot at Williams Air Force Base in Arizona in 1977. Mike was a member of the senior class, or the class that started six months ahead of me. Mike was easy to relate to. He had entered pilot training a little later than those of us who had entered training from the academy because Mike was already a captain.

Though Mike was friendly, he kept me at a distance. He also kept my good friend who lived next to me at a distance. I found out later that Mike treated us this way because we were Christians. Every now and then Mike would make fun of us or crack a joke at our expense, but I didn't really think much about it.

Five years later, when Mike and I briefly crossed paths in Korea, he shared that he had become a Christian. His words encouraged me as we discussed his experiences since he'd left Williams Air Force Base.

Fifteen years after I had retired from the Air Force, Mike and his wife, Eve, traveled through Dayton, Ohio, where my family was living at the time. The couple was on their way to visit a church in a city a few miles north of us. After meeting in Korea, we'd kept in touch, so they knew we were living in Dayton.

During our lunch together, Mike shared with me that they were missionaries working in Indonesia for a Christian organization called JAARS, the Jungle Aviation and Radio Service. JAARS performs the very important task of providing safe and reliable air service to remote areas, and is essential to bringing various supplies, especially medical supplies, to these areas.

As a missionary pilot, Mike flies in heavy rainstorms and has to avoid typhoons, which are very common. Also, because of the rugged terrain in some places, the pilot must be very skillful to land on the grass strips that are not necessarily level or have a smooth surface. Missionary pilots provide a lifeline for other missionaries.

One very humbling story that Mike told was how his contact with me during pilot training greatly influenced him to become a Christian. He shared that as he watched my friend John and me interact with each other, he saw that we were different than most of the others around him. Mike commented that when he became a Christian, he then understood why John and I were different and that our example really helped him along the path of putting his faith in Jesus Christ.

Because of his strong spiritual convictions, when Mike resigned from the Air Force, he decided to raise all his children in another country as he and Eve served on the mission field. Mike's children grew up in Indonesia. This was a total commitment. The children helped with all aspects of the mission work along with his wife, who specializes in linguistics or in communicating between different cultures.

Though they are not Wycliffe Bible Translators, they serve in a similar organization that is also focused on making sure the indigenous people in a particular area have the Word of God in their language. Eve writes curriculum and helps teach children in the village other school subjects, as well.

Mike spent about ten years in the Air Force fulfilling the five-year commitment required after completing Pilot Training. Once he separated from the Air Force, his faith led to a call to go on the mission field and raise his family there. America continues to send out the bulk of cross-cultural missionaries, and it is a testament to its peoples' dedication to the value of faith that this is so.

## Extraordinary MKs

To give more insight into the commitment Mike and Eve Brooks made to raise their children in another country on the mission field, here are some insights gained from some of my International School of Bangkok (ISB) friends who were missionary kids (MKs) during the late 1960s and 1970s. These friends lived with their parents in various countries in Asia like Burma, Vietnam, Malaysia, Bangladesh, and upcountry Thailand. When the country their parents were serving in as missionaries became too violent due to internal strife or all-out warfare, or when my friends advanced to a certain point academically in school where their parents decided to no longer homeschool them, they were sent to Bangkok to live in a hostel with other missionary kids. Their hostel parents served as their surrogate moms and dads.

Slightly different than Mike and Eve Brooks, the parents of my friends usually felt the calling to make missionary work their life's work when they were very young. One of my friends told me that each of her parents had decided to go on the mission field in high school before they even met. Years of education and training were required before the missionaries were sent to another country. Though they might have the desire to serve God in a specific country, the church denomination mission board determined where they were sent. So, in some instances, their children might be born in the country where they were serving outside of the United States.

My MK friends were very resourceful. Most of them did very well academically, a testament to the high quality of homeschooling they received. It was not uncommon for some of them to attend an Ivy League school upon graduating from high school. This was many years ago when attending an Ivy League school meant much more than it does today. A few of them were my track and field teammates.

When I was senior class president, one of my MK friends was the class secretary. In any case, I knew many of them well. One of the things that they all said when we reconnected later in life was that growing up away from their families and living in a hostel was difficult. Most of them really liked the country they lived in where their parents served, so coming to Bangkok may not necessarily have been what they wanted to do. This sentiment is also related to not having a hometown especially in the United States.

Most of us who went to high school overseas experienced culture shock when we returned to the United States to attend college. My observation is that some of my MK friends might have felt more culture shock than others because many of them lived most of their lives outside of the United States, even though they visited during regularly scheduled furloughs.

An example of this cultural disconnect concerns a time when one of my MK friends approached me at the end of our senior year just before we graduated, asked me not to laugh, showed me a picture of a snow-covered landscape, and asked me how did snow fall. That question made me realize that this friend who had lived in Thailand up to that day was about to spend a significant amount of time in college in an amazing country with which he was almost entirely unfamiliar. I felt sad.

Some of the professions my MK friends entered into were teaching, engineering, chemistry, business, and serving God as pastors or in other capacities related to church service. Not surprisingly, some also became missionaries in other countries. I have a very high regard for my MK friends. Knowing them enriched my life. I'm hoping this account gives some insight into the total commitment that American missionaries make to exercise their faith to serve God helping people around the world.

## BILLY KIM

When I was stationed in Korea from 1981 to 1984, I met a very inspiring Christian man by the name of Pastor Billy Kim, a Korean Baptist minister. I found the story of this man's early life in Korea compelling.

Billy Kim was born into a poor Korean family. During the Korean War, an American military man by the name of Sergeant Carl Powers took an interest in the little boy who did the housework and he decided to help raise him. After the war, Sergeant Powers guided Billy and provided the money necessary for him to attend college. Eventually Billy chose to go into the ministry.

After completing seminary, Billy Kim returned to Korea and pastored a church. I met Billy because he would preach once a month at the Osan Air Force Base Chapel in the afternoons, and I had the privilege of getting to know him well.

When I asked him why he came to the base to preach, he explained that the efforts of Sergeant Carl Powers had made it possible for him to advance in life, and in response, he had developed a great fondness for members of the U.S. military. Coming to preach at Osan Air Base was his way of honoring Sergeant Powers.

Due to Billy Kim's ability to preach well, he was chosen to translate for Billy Graham during his 1973 evangelistic crusade in Korea. Billy Kim is a powerful man of God, and his life is another example of the far-reaching and positive effect the American value of faith can have on people around the world.

## My Walk of Faith

Over the years, I saw the lives of other people changed by the Word of God. I've had the privilege of serving as a Deacon in Patterson Park Church, a nondenominational church located in Dayton, Ohio, where my family worshipped at various times over a twenty-year period as job requirements caused us to move to different cities. Later, I served as an elder in Redeemer Orthodox Presbyterian Church, also located in Dayton. Helping to guide families apply the Word of God to their lives and seeing the impact it had on helping them go through tough situations was a privilege. Watching the principles found in the Bible help children go forward in their lives and learn how to make wise decisions was encouraging, and it was an honor to serve others in this way.

Today my wife and I attend Grace Community Church, a Reformed Baptist Church, located in Minden, Nevada. Central to the lives of millions of Americans is the idea that faith or a belief in God is an American value that was woven into the fabric of America from the beginning. In most cases, those who deny this fact, or belittle faith in God, call out how there must be a complete "separation of church and state." Unfortunately, many Americans do not even know where this phrase originates. If asked, most answer, "Oh it's in the Constitution." Well, it's not.

## About the Demand for a "Separation of Church and State"

The concept of separation of church and state comes from a letter that Thomas Jefferson wrote to the Danbury Baptists, where he states:

> "...I contemplate with sovereign reverence that act of the whole American people which declared that their legislature should "make no law respecting an establishment of religion, or prohibiting the free exercise thereof," thus building a wall of separation between Church & State."[88]

Jefferson was serving as the third President of the United States at this time. In the early history of the United States, there were many different Christian groups seeking the ability to worship freely according to the dictates of their conscience. Lack of religious freedom is a major reason many groups left Europe, especially England, since the Anglican Church was decreed by the government to be the State religion, or religion of the country.[89] If you weren't Anglican, you would experience difficulties like the Anabaptists did during that time. The Anabaptists were persecuted, and some were killed, by both the Catholics and Lutherans because they were thought to be a threat to the social order.[90]

The Danbury Baptists wrote to Thomas Jefferson because they were concerned that the United States would develop a national religion like England had. Thomas Jefferson then wrote the famous line quoted above, that there would be a "wall of separation between Church and State."

Considering the context of this letter, "Church" is not thought of in the same way today. In the judicial and legislative bodies in the United States today the meaning is twisted to claim that no aspect of faith should have any influence on the state or federal government whatsoever. In the original context it is very clear that religious beliefs would have a profound influence on the state and federal government,[91] but there would be no one "Church" designated as the only one the government allowed or approved.

Our system of representative government was firmly based on the biblical view that man is flawed, and therefore, there must be checks and balances within the government. All men are answerable to God whether they believe in Him or not.[92] That's the basis of what our country was built on. So the wall of separation between church and state meant that the state was not allowed to interfere with the church.

It is perplexing today then, that we see the exact opposite in practice: there are dictates from the government telling churches how they must operate. The most recent glaring example was during the COVID-19 pandemic, when state governments determined whether churches could meet or not. This decision is outside the authority of the state or government. The separation of church and state meant we would not have a national church in America, and the state would not become involved or interfere with the operations of the church.

---

It is quite evident that faith is central to the proper governmental structure of the United States and that faith in a higher power is an American value. One thing that I remember from when I was very small living in Philadelphia is that in our neighborhood we had Protestants, and we had Catholics, and we had Jewish people, and there were other people of yet other faiths.

What was notable is that even though on the weekend we children ran around and had fun, our parents, especially my parents, would remind us that Saturday is the holy day for the Jewish people, so it was very important that we were careful not to be loud near their homes. And the holy day for the Protestants and the Catholics was Sunday. We were also told to be considerate on that day and not make as much noise as we usually did. It was a day of reflection.

> In summary, faith is important to America. It is an American value. And it is something that we need to pass on to those who come after us, to our children and then the next generations. A respect for faith is something that will hold our society together. Man is not the final authority over what is right and wrong. We determine what is moral from how we view ourselves in the world. When we view ourselves responsible to a higher power, there is a constraint that will make us act in a way that is responsible. If men think they are the ultimate authority, this is when the atrocities we have witnessed throughout history happen. Therefore, we must always champion faith as an American value.

# 7
## THE TRIBE

*"Behold, children are a heritage from the LORD,
the fruit of the womb a reward."*

—***Psalm 127:3 ESV***

When we became parents, Donna and I made a conscious effort to raise our children with an understanding of who God is, to be educated with the purpose of obtaining a job, to support themselves, and to always remember that they have a responsibility to contribute to society. To accomplish these principles, we focused on their spiritual development, education, and physical development. Donna and I are blessed that all of our children are accomplished.

Our four children—John, Jasmine, Holly, and Benjamin—are fine young men and women. They have initiative and pursue their goals. They support themselves and their families. They know who their Creator is. They are a blessing to Donna and me.

John graduated from the United States Naval Academy, Annapolis, Maryland, with a Bachelor of Science in Political Science. He chose to serve as a United States Marine Corps officer. John is a helicopter pilot and flew combat missions in Afghanistan.

Jasmine graduated with a Bachelor of Science in Molecular Biology from Westminster College in Pennsylvania. She also earned a Master of Arts in Bioethics and a Master of Arts in Teaching from Trinity International University in Deerfield, Illinois. She worked in laboratories and taught science to middle school and high school students.

Holly graduated with a Bachelor of Science in Athletic Training from Wilmington College in Ohio and a Master of Science in Sports Management from the University of Tennessee, Knoxville, Tennessee. She is an entrepreneur managing her own personal training business.

Benjamin graduated from the United States Military Academy, West Point, New York, with a Bachelor of Science in Mechanical Engineering. He also earned a Master of Science in Engineering Management from the Missouri University of Science and Technology, in Rolla, Missouri. He is serving as a United States Army officer.

## OUR FAMILY STORY

Since we are both Christians, Donna and I believe man is made in the image of God and therefore has dignity. We believe children are a blessing, and the family is the foundational basic unit of society. Children belong to their parents and not to society.

When Donna and I married at the United States Air Force Academy Chapel in 1983, we were of one mind spiritually. Our first child, John, was born in 1986 in Plattsburgh, New York. Both daughters were born in Dayton, Ohio, Jasmine in 1989 and Holly in 1990. Benjamin was born in Montgomery, Alabama, in 1992. The short six-year span between our four children caused them to be fairly cohesive growing up. This cohesiveness is why I call them "the tribe."

## SPIRITUAL DEVELOPMENT

We prayed for our children before they were born. We asked our family and friends for their prayers, also, so each of their births was an answer to prayer. From their earliest moments we took them to church with us which was an important part of our lives long before they were born, and the children became very familiar with the church environment as they grew up.

In some places we lived, we attended the Air Force Base Chapel. In others we attended church in the local community. As they grew older the children would attend Sunday School to learn Bible verses and biblical principles. The AWANA organization was very helpful for their spiritual growth. As mentioned in Chapter 6, AWANA is a Christian organization which stands for Approved Workmen Are Not Ashamed, a paraphrase of the Bible verse 2 Timothy 2:15. Children from ages 2 to 18 participate in this program. AWANA helps disciple, or train, children's minds and make positive impressions on them as they memorize passages from the Bible, which is the Word of God.

As a family, we had regular evening devotions where a Bible passage or a story with a Christian theme was read. Then we prayed together before the children went to bed.

Other spiritual development opportunities included mission trips. While they were in high school, both Holly and Jasmine took part in these trips visiting Mexico. The desire to share the Word of God with people in other countries continues with Holly today, as she has made multiple short-term trips to Romania to assist missionaries working full time there. Benjamin participated in local mission efforts in downtown Dayton, Ohio, through his Boy Scout Troop by working in a kitchen to feed the homeless. These activities taught the children to be mindful of the needs of others, especially since all men are made in the image of God.

When the children were older, I studied the Bible with them individually, and I assigned a few books for them to read by Christian authors to help them further understand spiritual principles. John, Jasmine, and Holly had additional spiritual input because they attended private Christian schools that required them to spend time reading their Bibles, memorizing, and reciting verses.

Donna and I also sent them to attend Summit Ministries, a Christian organization located in Manitou Springs, Colorado. Summit prepares Christian children for the attacks on the Christian Worldview that they will experience in college. Training at Summit equipped them to stand firm in their faith.

## Discipline Policies

Though we desired the best for our children, raising them was very difficult at times. Donna and I were not our children's friends, we were their parents. Both of us were carefully disciplined growing up. We disciplined our children the same way. We believe the Bible which states, "Folly is bound up in the heart of a child, but the rod of discipline drives it far from him." Proverbs 22:15 ESV, and "Do not withhold discipline from a child; if you strike him with a rod, he will not die." Proverbs 23:13 ESV.

We set the standard of conduct for our children. Once, when we were traveling between Air Force assignments, we spent the night in a Holiday Inn located in Kingman, Arizona. In the morning, we ate at the breakfast buffet in the dining room. After we finished eating, I went to the cash register to pay, and the lady at the register said that she was the manager and was concerned when our family entered the room with four small children. She went on to say she was pleasantly surprised with how well they behaved. I smiled and said that we love our children and take them everywhere we go. We do not let them misbehave at home when they are eating, so when we go to restaurants, we certainly do not allow them to act differently. She was amazed.

On another occasion, right before I picked up John from his high school team basketball practice, the coach walked up to me and said, "Thank you for spanking him when he was younger." I looked surprised and asked, "How can you tell?" He just replied, "Oh I can tell. It is very clear which of the boys were spanked when they were growing up, and which ones weren't." So, we were careful to raise our children to meet the behavior standard that we set, though at times, it was very difficult.

Of course, we were not perfect, since Donna and I are flawed human beings. But God does not require parents to be perfect, that would be impossible. He asks them to be faithful and raise their children in the fear and admonition of the Lord Jesus Christ. This we did to the best of our abilities despite our flaws. We stood in the gap for them between the evil that is present throughout the world and the promise of eternal life given by the Lord Jesus Christ.

We raised our children to conform to the Word of God, which they have benefited from throughout their lives. Though there were times in the past, especially when they were in high school, that the children pushed back against us as parents, it is encouraging today when we hear from them multiple times, "Thank you for raising me this way."

## Education

Prior to leaving Plattsburgh Air Force Base, before John was born, I became aware of The Institutes for the Achievement of Human Potential, located in Philadelphia, Pennsylvania. The nickname for this institution is The Better Baby Institutes. It was founded by Glenn Doman in 1955.

Doman and George S. Patton served together as platoon leaders during the First World War. His relationship with the famous General certainly caught my attention because I was a budding Air Force Officer eager to learn from those who made an impact on the world especially through successful military action.

Since my parents lived in Philadelphia, I took the opportunity to visit the Institutes. Their main focus was helping severely brain-injured children develop as much as possible to be able to function in life. The Institutes were able to help some of these children to come out of their comas.

An unintended byproduct of their research was that they discovered many important ways that the brain learns. This discovery occurred (despite their low success rate in the overall number of brain-injured children they were able to return to normalcy) when a significant number of the children that they were able to help began to out-perform peers (both academically and physically) who had not experienced any brain injuries. In their extensive analysis they discovered how the brain takes in and uses information.

A key person who assisted the Institutes was Dr. Temple Fay, who established the Department of Neurosurgery at Temple University Hospital, Philadelphia, in 1930.[93] He was also a professor of neurology.[94] To fund part of their brain injury research, the university hospital created a program for well kids, where The Better Baby Institutes would train parents how to teach their children.

One of the profound lessons I learned attending their courses is that from birth to six years old is the time when the human brain can take information in the fastest. After six years old the rate at which the brain learns begins to decrease.[95] This revolutionized my thinking about education. In the United States most formal learning may not even start until a child is six years old, so Donna and I started applying these teaching techniques to our children when they were babies.

When teaching babies, parents must learn that you will not necessarily see any results for a long while. This delay can be discouraging sometimes. John was two years old at Edwards Air Force Base before we noticed a response. He was a very quiet baby and rarely spoke.

One day, when I came home from classes at the Test Pilot School located at the base, Donna was extremely excited. She shared with me that John was out in the yard putting rocks in his mouth as toddlers often do. As she leaned down to take the rocks out of his mouth, she could hear him counting. This surprised her. John was counting the rocks. We then realized that he was learning the information that we were trying to teach him.

At Test Pilot School during certain flights, the aircraft flew fast enough to break the sound barrier which creates a shock wave. People on the ground hear the shock wave as a sonic boom. It sounds like thunder and can cause buildings in its path to shake. When it creates a shock wave, an aircraft is flying supersonic. If the fast-flying aircraft is low enough to the ground, the shock wave makes a rather loud sonic boom and can be strong enough to break windows and knock small slightly-built structures over.

The supersonic corridor is an area in the air, or airspace, where airplanes are allowed to intentionally fly supersonic by Federal Aviation Regulations. These corridors are established high enough to prevent supersonic flights from damaging anything on the ground. At Edwards Air Force Base, this corridor stretches across the sky high above the base housing area.

One of my favorite memories is coming home and hearing my very quiet two-year-old son say, "Sonic boom, daddy, go sonic boom today," because all the houses on the block shook slightly when he heard the thunder caused by the flying plane. Weeks before, Donna had explained to him about sonic booms and what was sometimes happening when I flew a plane overhead.

Some of the teaching techniques involved showing the children rather large words written in two-inch letters and numbers represented by groups of dots on cards we made out of posterboard. Also, we showed them pictures or images mounted on 11-inch x 11-inch posterboard squares in rapid succession. The children would brighten up when we showed them these items.

Another area of education that we adopted from The Better Baby Institutes was exposing our children to music. We had all of them take violin lessons. We started them between two and four years old depending on when the individual child was ready. The intent was to give them an appreciation for music.

We used the Suzuki method. This teaching method, sometimes called the mother tongue method, requires the parent work with the child every day. The teacher only sees the child once a week. Their first lessons lasted for about five minutes, then progressed to fifteen minutes. Eventually they lasted for a maximum of thirty minutes.

The violin was a good instrument for our purposes, as it is small and easy to travel with. We found a music shop from which we could rent violins in Dayton, Ohio, which provided larger violins as the children's bodies grew larger.

About this time Donna and I decided to homeschool because I was reaching the point in my Air Force career where we would be moving often. John was the first to start a structured curriculum. Both sets of our parents thought we had gone mad and were not happy with our decision. We made this choice well before home schooling was widely accepted as a useful method for education.

We obtained our curriculum from the Calvert School, which is located in Baltimore, Maryland. Because everything you needed for each lesson came in a box including pens, pencils, and paper in addition to the textbooks, we called it "school in a box."

We also used their additional program where Calvert teachers would grade the children's tests and return them to us with comments.

With this service, the Calvert School kept records of our children's progress, so if we decided in the future to put them in regular school, they would have records like any other student that might have transferred from another school.

After two years, the Air Force assigned me to Maxwell AFB, Montgomery, Alabama, and we continued our school program there. Finding a violin teacher in Montgomery was a challenge though. The closest teacher who taught the Suzuki method was too far away in Auburn, so I called the Montgomery symphony orchestra to see if they could help me out.

To our surprise, the newly hired concert master, Andy Simionescu, who had just moved to Montgomery from New York, offered to take on John as a student. John enjoyed his weekly thirty-minute lessons with Andy. Andy didn't use the Suzuki method, but we maintained this teaching format at home.

Though Donna, who is musically inclined, started as the parent teacher with John, when Holly came along, I became John's teacher while Donna juggled the two baby girls. I am not musically inclined with any instrument. The beauty of the Suzuki method is that the parent does not need to be good, just consistent. Very soon, John sounded much better than I did.

After Andy worked with him for two years, John sounded wonderful! As part of Andy Simionescu's contract with the Montgomery Symphony Orchestra, he played four recitals a year. Before we left Montgomery, Andy had John play on stage in front of the audience before he started his recital.[96]

John was six years old. He did a superb job and was given a very nice review in the newspaper by the music critic who attended the recital.[97]

After living in Montgomery, Alabama, for two years, the Air Force assigned me to the Pentagon, so our family moved to Washington, D.C., and lived on Bolling Air Force Base. In Washington, D.C., because there were many home school groups, we had an encouraging support system where the children participated in many group activities.

After eighteen months, the Air Force sent us back to Edwards Air Force Base, but, once again, moving didn't deter us. Shortly after we arrived, Jasmine began to play the violin and soon after Holly joined her, and we continued to follow The Better Baby techniques with the younger three.

After three years, I retired from the Air Force, so we left Edwards Air Force Base and returned to Dayton, Ohio. I had been hired by FedEx and could commute from Dayton to Memphis, Tennessee, for training.

Once I'd completed training, I volunteered to fly out of Subic Bay, Philippines, the original Asian Hub of operations for FedEx. I chose this location to give my children an opportunity to live in another country. I wanted them to see what other cultures were like and compare those other cultures to the United States.

The whole family embraced living in the Philippines. The children especially enjoyed watching the monkeys try to get into our garbage cans that were bound with industrial strength bungee cords. By this time, all the children were enrolled in the Calvert School curriculum, and all four also played the violin. We traveled from Subic Bay to Manila once a week to work with their violin teacher.

John was able to join an American Boy Scout Troop in Manila. I accompanied the Troop on many campouts with him. During our time in the Philippines, we traveled to Singapore for a vacation. The trip gave the children the opportunity to visit an additional country and experience yet another culture.

While in the Philippines our children met children from many different countries. Getting to know more about the lives of these children was a valuable experience for them. After a year in the Philippines, our family returned to Dayton, Ohio, and I was domiciled out of Memphis, Tennessee, continuing to fly FedEx airplanes around the world.

After ten moves, eight while in the Air Force and two with FedEx, Donna and I chose to anchor the family in Dayton, Ohio. We based this decision on our earlier experience living there when we'd found it to be a very nice city with friendly people, and we wanted to provide a consistent environment to prepare our four well for college. It was a good place to raise our children.

An added benefit was that we could drive to both of our parents' homes in a reasonable amount of time. This geographical advantage kept Donna and me out of trouble because it allowed us to visit both sets of grandparents regularly. My parents lived in Albrightsville, located in the Poconos in Pennsylvania, and Donna's parents lived in Powell, Tennessee, located just outside of Knoxville. By this time our parents began to be more supportive of our decision to home school our children as they watched them grow and develop in a positive way.

Once back in Dayton, it was time for John to enter high school. All along Donna and I had planned to place the children in high school so they would experience being in a classroom environment before pursuing the rest of their formal education. We wanted them to be comfortable and to know how to excel outside of home school.

We enrolled John in Dayton Christian High School for his freshman year. Jasmine also attended Dayton Christian High School when she finished the Calvert curriculum. Holly attended Xenia Christian High School. In Dayton, Donna taught Benjamin with the K-12 curriculum developed by Bill Bennett, the former U.S. Secretary of Education,[98] until Benjamin completed eighth grade. Then he was enrolled in Beavercreek High School, a local public school.

Though the children had other activities that they participated in, it is noteworthy that John enjoyed acting in the school theater productions. Benjamin was on the Speech and Debate team. He also participated in theater and enjoyed making movies with one of his friends who wrote the scripts. We were pleased with all of our children's schools.

One interesting memory I have about the children's thoughts on home schooling is that throughout learning at home, all of them had asked to go to regular school rather than stay home. Yet when they finally attended regular school, within about a month, they wanted to return to home schooling.

They realized in the traditional school setting, much time was wasted compared to what they'd experienced while being taught at home. In home school they were motivated to finish their lessons because when they were finished, they could use their free time to do what they wanted. They discovered very quickly that this formula for getting free time did not exist in traditional schools. They were required to remain in the classroom until they were dismissed, regardless of whether or not they completed their work.

Donna and I were actively involved with the education of our children. We experienced public and private schools with three of our children attending private high schools and one of them a public high school. Donna worked tirelessly while home schooling them although at times teaching the children was very difficult for her.

One of the many benefits of working with The Better Baby Institutes is that we became aware of unique conditions related to each of our children that we might not have known if they attended public or private school.

Three of them were not reading as well as we thought they should. When we consulted the Institutes, they suggested that we take the children to the optometrist. He analyzed the situation and prescribed mild strength reading glasses.

This action quickly solved the problem. The children's reading skills improved almost immediately. The doctor advised us that one of the children would grow out of wearing glasses, which happened in less than a year. The others wore them only at certain times. We are thankful that we received such excellent advice that helped our children to learn.

Once they were in high school, I met most of my children's teachers and all of their principals and guidance counselors. I knew first-hand how each child was doing in school and what their school environment was like. My understanding of what was going on and the people who had authority helped our children to be successful in high school. A math teacher informed us that one of our children had stopped turning in homework. We saw to it that this behavior was corrected immediately. On another occasion, another child was experiencing particular difficulty in memorizing state capitals and other unique features of each state. Donna and I were able to zero in on this problem and work together with the child to bring about greatly improved performance. Success in high school formed a solid and critical foundation for them to stand on when they attended college.

Our children chose their colleges to pursue their individual goals. Many people ask how I talked my boys into attending military service academies and are surprised to find out that I didn't. In fact, I tried to talk both of them out of going to a service academy.

Because I had graduated from the Air Force Academy, I knew what they were going to experience, so I made sure they understood what they were getting themselves into. Both boys are exceptionally bright and perform well academically. However, because of their stated interests and temperaments, I did not want them to start down a path that they might regret in the future.

One child had authority issues. I did not want him to enter the highly regimented environment of a service academy and become frustrated with the rigid hierarchal structure. The other child showed a strong interest in becoming an attorney. In my opinion there were much better schools to attend to pursue this career field. Also, I thought that by the time he might become a military attorney, a Judge Advocate General or JAG, that he might be limited in the area of law that he might be able to practice.

However, both of them wanted to attend, because they wanted to serve the country. They think the United States is a great country and worth defending. So, the boys attended the academies for the right reasons. Their patriotism and commitment are why they graduated successfully and are serving the country now as military commissioned officers.

The girls each had their own approach to selecting a college. Jasmine likes science and pursued molecular biology. She eventually discovered that she liked teaching and became a science teacher. She works very well with children.

Holly likes sports and decided she wanted to become an athletic trainer. She chose Wilmington College because it was one of the top colleges in the United States to study athletic training. Another benefit was students traveled each year to see how athletic training was performed in other countries. Holly continued to travel after graduation and even spent a year living in New Zealand while pursuing more experience in Athletic Training.

Donna and I are proud of our children's pursuits in education and the way they have become self-supporting in the careers they chose.

## PHYSICAL DEVELOPMENT

The Better Baby Institutes also emphasized physical development. Both Donna and I played sports in college. I was a Division I Track & Field athlete at the Air Force Academy, and Donna played club soccer at Texas A & M. It was natural for us to see the importance of making sure that our children became physically fit.

One of the not-so-common items used for physical development as well as brain development suggested by The Better Baby Institutes even for very young children was monkey bars. I built and mounted them inside our house.

At various stages in their abilities, we would hold our children up to grab the bars until they became strong enough to jump up and grab the bars by themselves. Eventually they would swing from rung to rung and have lots of fun. When people visited us, they thought it strange to see monkey bars inside of our house. Donna and I chuckled when this happened.

John hanging on the first monkey bars I built while sitting on my shoulder. This photo was taken in the hallway of our house on Plattsburg Air Force Base, located in upstate New York in 1987. John was one year old. The monkey bars help the child develop his breathing and assist in brain development by sharpening eye-hand coordination.

John and Jasmine on the monkey bars I built to stand alone and can be adjusted to match the height of the child. In this photo the bars are adjusted for Jasmine's height. This photo was taken in our house located in Dayton, Ohio, in 1991. John is five years old and Jasmine is two years old.

When we lived in the Philippines when the children were still very young, we needed to work out in the morning before it became too hot. I'd continued my personal workout routine that I'd developed over the years. The children had watched me run and accomplish calisthenics in the morning before breakfast from when they were babies. When they came along, my routine consisted of stretching, one set of 100 continuous push-ups, 100 continuous sit-ups, a three-mile run, and warm down stretches. Sometimes, I would swim continuously for a mile to break up the routine.

I exercised four to five days a week. Because I'd modeled this routine, the children considered exercise as a normal personal activity. We trained as a family to eventually run three miles in thirty minutes at the time the children were ages six to twelve. I'd made a practice of exercising with each child separately until he or she was about six years old, but in the Philippines, we were able to all work out together because Benjamin had reached the age of six.

## AMERICAN VALUES: ANOTHER VOICE

This emphasis on physical exercise developed the discipline in each child to workout regularly. Each of our children learned to take responsibility for his or her own physical fitness. They played on their school sports teams when they were in high school. John was a track and field team member and also played on the basketball and soccer teams. Jasmine ran track and cross country. Holly played tennis, soccer, and basketball. Benjamin played soccer, ran track his senior year, and then participated in a community basketball league.

In college, John was on the Naval Academy track and field team. Jasmine was on the Westminster College track and cross-country teams. Holly played on the Wilmington College tennis team. Benjamin played intramurals at West Point. I had the privilege of coaching all of my children in track and field. Because they all became athletes, my children have a lifestyle of staying in shape today.

> God blessed Donna and me with four healthy children. Because of our Christian faith, we believed it was our responsibility to raise our children well because they are a gift from God. We purposed to train them spiritually to know who God is, help them to become educated, and create in them a habit of seeking to be physically fit. Through their initiative, our children have taken what we taught them and are supporting themselves and their families and are contributing to society. This outcome is a blessing.

# 8
# WHERE I STAND

*"Here I stand, I can do no other, so help me God. Amen."*
—**Martin Luther,** *Priest, before the Diet (Assembly) of Worms, April 18, 1521*

From the time I was seven years old when my father's job working for the United Nations took our family to Lagos, Nigeria, to living in Thailand, eventually graduating from high school there, to serving in the U.S. Air Force, to flying FedEx airplanes around the world, I have had a life of service representing the United States of America. I have also served my local communities by coaching track, being a scoutmaster, and filling the position of Air Boss or Director of Flight Operations/Race Director for the National Championship Reno Air Races. Doing these things has been my privilege.

Many complain about the government; well, I decided to do something about it. I ran to become the Lieutenant Governor of Nevada in 2022 in order to serve the citizens of this great state. I won thirteen of seventeen counties, but was edged out by 5.8% in the June Primary. I learned much from that race and am glad that I went through the campaign. I feel good about living a life of service to others in my country and in my community.

AMERICAN VALUES: ANOTHER VOICE

# I AM A PROUD AMERICAN

The United States is a sovereign nation. We fought the Revolutionary War to create it, the Civil War to preserve it, and two world wars to stand against those who would try to dominate it. Borders mean something. They are established to clearly let others around the world know the specific geographical area a nation's government controls.

I am a proud American since I had the opportunity to also grow up overseas living in and visiting other countries. I became very patriotic realizing that the United States is the greatest country on the face of the earth. I know this country is worth the twenty years I served in the Air Force defending and preserving it.

As an Air Force officer, I swore an oath to "support and defend the Constitution of the United States against all enemies foreign and domestic."[99] Military members view service before self is necessary to preserve something greater than themselves. It was my honor to join with those who have gone before me and sacrificed so that Americans can live well.

It was my honor to serve this great county as a U.S. Air Force pilot. I also became a test pilot and assisted in the process of fielding new weapons. I participated in developing new airplanes so that America remains vigilant by staying on the cutting-edge of advanced technology and applying it to defend our nation. "For those who have fought for it, freedom has a special flavor the protected will never know."[100]

**I believe in the American values on which this country was built.** They form the bedrock and fundamental foundation of this great nation. They include virtue, strength of character, liberty, and faith. These values make families stronger and have bound Americans together as a people throughout the past two hundred and forty-eight years, regardless of who they might be or where they came from.

Most Americans have always honored these values, though a few have not. Unfortunately, at times some of those few held positions of power where their un-American ideas were magnified when imposed on the entire country. Ideas do have consequences.[101]

My parents instilled these American values in me. They are my compass that successfully navigated me through life. These values come from what is enshrined in the Declaration of Independence and the Constitution, namely, the unalienable rights of Life, Liberty, and the Pursuit of Happiness: the rule of law, freedom,[102] individual responsibility, fiscal responsibility, and doing what is right.

**As a constitutional originalist, I believe that the words as they were originally written in the document mean what they say.** The words are specific and precise and are not open to broad interpretation. The Constitution is not a living breathing document; it does not need to be reinterpreted for the current times. This document is the supreme law of the land and has a built-in method for change through the amendment process,[103] which is the only method through which the Constitution was intended to be changed, and change would come because the will of the people demanded it. In this way slavery was abolished in our country, voting was expanded and then the right of women to vote was recognized—all implemented by amending the Constitution.

The framers of the Constitution did not believe in judicial review or the courts determining if an issue was constitutional.[104] Modern courts gained this power though nibbling away at the precepts of the Constitution by establishing legal precedent through Judicial activism. The original purpose of the courts was to make sure that the constitutional principles were upheld in the application of the law in any case brought before them. The 3/5ths clause dealing with Black slaves[105] was a compromise reached through political maneuvering and expediency to keep from losing the main objective of ratifying a constitution to govern an emerging nation and hold it together.[106]

The beginning of the first sentence of the Constitution, "We the people of the United States, in order to form a ***more perfect*** union..." [emphasis added] states clearly that the framers had not necessarily achieved all that they wanted, but what they did achieve was better than any method of governing that existed at that time. The rule of law is the basis for all transactions, contract law, and protection of personal property; it does not change on a whim. If it did, no one could ever be certain that the terms of any contract they signed would be followed.

**I believe in the sanctity of life because I believe in the dignity of every human being, from conception through natural death and all periods of human existence in between.** I stand here because all men are made in the image of God, and all men as His image bearers must be treated with respect. This goal has not always been what people have carried out in our society and that is why we must be vigilant to keep moving toward this ideal.

**I believe in fiscal responsibility.** You cannot pay for something if you lack the money to buy it, and using debt to buy everything is not a useful long-term financial strategy. Sound financial discipline is the only way to pass on the opportunity of a bright future to our children and grandchildren. We should not pass on to them a large debt burden that they must shoulder.

**I believe in limited government, a government to serve not to dictate to the people.** The government exists to provide all citizens with opportunity by making sure that laws are applied to everyone equally and to keep the nation safe. It is not the government's job to take care of every aspect of a person's life.

**I believe in self-determination.** No American should be placed in an arbitrary category due to some innate characteristic, like skin color, which has nothing to do with a person's character or who that person really is.

**I believe our borders should keep illegal aliens out.** If the border is not enforced, you do not have a country.

**I believe in free speech, the right to bear arms, and freedom of religion.**

**I believe freedom is an unalienable right, meaning that the rights that come with freedom cannot be taken away from the American people.** Rights are given by God, not by other men, but by God Almighty. This concept is what the authors of the Declaration of Independence and the framers of the Constitution believed, whether they were members of a particular religious denomination or not. All of them believed that all men are responsible to a higher power. The Declaration of Independence recognizes that these rights were given by God and the purpose of government is to defend these rights.[107]

# A SAMPLING OF CURRENT POLITICAL HOT BUTTON ISSUES

## FAMILY

The family is the basic unit of our nation. Strong families make strong communities, strong communities make strong cities, strong cities make strong states, and those strong states make a great nation. And so, the family must be supported and protected so it will thrive and shall not to be dictated to. The government does not own children; children belong to the family. The government is there to ensure the laws are equally administered to everyone and not to intervene and tell parents how to raise their children. On these basic, easy-to-grasp ideas concerning "Family," I stand.

## SCHOOL CHOICE

American families should have school choice when seeking out education, not mandatory indoctrination. God blessed us with four children. It was our privilege to raise them. They are all successful in their chosen area of interest.

We used several methods to educate them prior to college. My wife homeschooled them through eighth grade, then three attended Christian private schools and one attended a public high school. Each attended the college of their choice. We emphasized that in whatever they do, that they do their best.

We are fortunate that they were taught in school and not indoctrinated. Our children had the liberty to pursue their interests without being told what they could or could not do or what they should think. Donna, my bride of forty years, and I are very proud of them. We believe that all parents should have the opportunity to choose where their children are educated.

## **MERITOCRACY**

The United States is a meritocracy although many today are trying to destroy this concept. When children compete in a school sport, some push the idea that there is no winner or loser. When the game is over everyone receives a trophy so that they won't feel left out. Teaching them to accept this incorrect idea hurts our children. It does not reflect reality.

Every professional sports team is ranked from best to worst. Only the best athletes are chosen for a team. Only the best team at the end of the season wins the title. Why is it important which football team wins the Superbowl in the NFL? Why does a basketball team win the NBA Championship? In hockey, why is the Stanley Cup given to the team that wins the playoffs? Because of meritocracy.

Americans enjoy competition. They want to see winners! If we do not allow children to learn this fact early in life, their viewpoints will be permanently hindered regarding competition as they grow older. It is important to experience losing sometimes to spark the drive to try harder next time.

Those who work the hardest usually win is a very important life lesson for children to learn; so we need to oppose those who do not believe in meritocracy. When it is necessary to have surgery, patients look for the doctor with the best results, not the one with the worst. We seek the best because it really matters.

I myself depended on the fairness of merit when I applied to the United States Air Force Academy located in Colorado Springs for college. It was an excellent school. The Academy looked for well-rounded applicants to select from. The cadets came from all areas of the country and from families up and down the economic ladder. There were cadets from small towns and big cities. Some even came from farms and other rural areas.

But though the cadets in my class were a very diverse group, there was one thing I knew we all shared. All of us met the requirements for entry to the Air Force Academy. We all met the required high standards, as anyone who failed to meet them was not chosen to attend the institution. Unity, respect, and trust were strong because of meritocracy. We had all earned entry and no one gave it to any of us.

## Marxism in "Progressive" Clothing

Today the Progressive Movement has developed three tools to promote change in American Society. Before discussing Critical Race Theory (CRT); Intersectionality; and Diversity Equity and Inclusion (DEI), it is necessary to establish a common point of understanding of the political philosophy behind these approaches to changing American society. The following is a brief discussion of the theory of Marxism, how Antonio Gramsci modified it to attack western societies, and especially how the detrimental changes we see happening in the United States today gained such popularity.

## A Brief History of American Marxism

Karl Marx, who never worked a day in his life at a real job to support himself, was financially supported by Friedrich Engels.[108] Marx's philosophy forms the basis for the leftwing political movement attacking the United States today. It was the leftwing political system that the Soviet Union embraced, and yet today that union is gone, firmly deposited in the dustbin of history where it belongs.

Marxism is the system that Venezuela follows, and that country is a nightmare with rampant inflation leading to spiraling economic decline[109] resulting in widespread poverty.[110] The principles of Marxism also inform Socialism.[111] John Mackey, the CEO of the very successful Whole Foods Market, the largest American chain of supermarkets specializing in natural and organic foods, commented that Socialist governments have been attempted forty-two times throughout the last 100 years and have failed every time.[112]

Marxism is based on three major principles: Atheism, Economic Determinism, and Class Struggle. In its atheistic worldview there is no higher power; man came into being through evolution, and the only thing that exists is the material or physical world around us.[113] Man is the supreme divinity and is basically good with any faults caused by an oppressive society. In Marxism, there are no absolutes because man and society are continually evolving.[114]

Economic determinism comes to be when the material or physical world is ordered by society through the means of production.[115] Society forms the values that determine how things are produced, instead of values forming the society that develops the production plan. Predictably, class struggle is ubiquitous after that because owners oppress workers, the essential part of production.

Through this class struggle, the workers will eventually throw off the yoke of the oppressors and eliminate social classes through the dictatorship of the proletariat who are enlightened leaders. This type of governing is socialism, but socialism is merely a way station on the path to somewhere else.

In socialism the government controls the means of production within society. The dictatorship of the proletariat will remain until a classless society evolves and then the dictatorship of the proletariat disappears because there is no need for it anymore. When this happens all means of production are equally owned by everyone, surpluses exist so that the needs of all are met, and a utopia known as communism is achieved.[116] In communism the government owns the means of production. But since everyone is the government, there is no need for a government per se because as the Marxists firmly predict, "the state withers away."[117]

So that sequence of milestones is supposed to happen.

Italian socialist Antonio Gramsci, however, fretted that the economic determinism of Marxism was not taking hold in the West after the Bolshevik Revolution (1917-1921) in Russia that formed the Soviet Union, because the workers in the West were content. They had plenty of food to eat and good living conditions. He theorized that the foundational institutions in the West that formed the society were the problem because they strengthened or held the society together and therefore needed to be destroyed.[118]

These institutions include, but are not limited to: churches, philanthropic foundations, media, schools, universities, and economic corporate powers. He targeted these institutions to be taken over by socialist thinkers who would then use them to revolutionize society.

The result of that takeover is what we see today in the United States. Many of our institutions have been taken over by those who are hostile to American values.[119] They are hostile to the American values that formed this great county because their bankrupt Marxist worldview directly conflicts with these values.

The framers of the Constitution and the Declaration of Independence, our foundational documents, believed in a higher power to whom man was responsible. They believed man was not basically good, but flawed, so government was formed with checks and balances. They established a society based on the rule of law to protect individual property rights.

The early American settlers in 1620 initially based society on all the members owning the means of production in common instead of individual ownership. This arrangement resulted in a disaster. Many starved to death![120] So, settlers quickly changed to individual ownership and thrived.

---

## CRT AND ITS GANG OF FRIENDS

Critical Race Theory (CRT); Intersectionality; and Diversity, Equity and Inclusion (DEI), disregard and are hostile to American values on which the United States was formed. By design, they divide instead of unify the citizens. They also disregard human nature and the rule of law. They are all rebranded Marxism that has been tried numerous times, only to fail miserably every time at tremendous human cost during the twentieth century.[121]

CRT is an academic theory that began in 1989.[122] It is a direct result of Antonio Gramsci's goal to attack the basic institutions of Western Society. It is Marxism rebranded in that it labels all Whites as oppressors,[123] and all Blacks and other minorities as oppressed or victims.[124] The advocates of this theory use language to hide the true Marxist ideology behind this theory.[125] This language includes terms such as equity, social justice, diversity and inclusion, and culturally responsive teaching.

Though these terms do not sound threatening, CRT advocates use them to attack fundamental American values. For example, though equity sounds like it is related to equality, it is far from it. Equality under the law is a principle found in the U.S. Constitution in the 14th and 15th Amendments. However, equity in CRT means, as one example, using the power of government through an unelected newly established department to take property or resources from one group—the dominant group, or Whites—and giving it to other non-White minorities or persons of color to balance racism which has occurred in the past.[126]

It is definitely against American values to take personal property away from someone without due process. But then Marxists do not believe in personal property rights, so this is perfectly acceptable to them.

Another term is diversity, which most people would agree is a good thing to have people of various backgrounds and viewpoints within an organization. But those pushing CRT, DEI, and Intersectionality only expect diversity to be about having people on their side of the political spectrum of different skin colors or ethnic backgrounds in the organization. If you point out to them that there are no conservatives or people who do not agree with Marxism in the mix, they will scream bloody murder and attempt to shut you down by calling you a racist or bigot.

There is no place for differing viewpoints in their world. They do not believe in free speech which is one of every American's basic Constitutional rights. They believe only in speech they allow, and they do not want to have debates.[127] Censorship of differing opinions is not an American value.

CRT spreads in businesses and other institutions through mandatory seminars (usually conducted by Human Resources), conferences, school curricula, and even mandatory government programs and regulations in the military.[128] It is tantamount to the tried-and-true practice of re-education for the mature and indoctrination for the children of the Communists in the former Soviet Union.

Intersectionality is a method of further dividing people in what are termed "marginalized groups" from the dominant group (the White people) by focusing on the different spheres of victimization or discrimination those in marginalized groups supposedly suffer.[129] These types of claimed victimization or discrimination are then highlighted as proof the dominant group is profoundly guilty and needs to be chastised by society as a whole.

An example of this would be if a homeless person is a minority and a female, the Marxist focus would solely be on her victimization due to her skin color and gender ignoring any other external reasons for her homelessness and not allowing any thought as to possible root causes of why she might be homeless. An insidious ingredient in the intersectionality formula is that her victimization must be automatically accepted as true and require no proof.

She might have mental illness; she might not have any marketable skills in demand where she lives; she might have had a recent traumatic experience that may have led to her homelessness. Determining the actual reasons she is homeless requires more effort than zeroing in on whatever ways a person could be viewed as a victim of some kind of discrimination. Intersectionality is yet another Marxist political tool to further divide the citizens of our country with the objective of creating conflict and no intention of solving problems that can be real and do need solutions.

DEI, developed out of CRT, can be considered a refined result of it. It is not enough to just have diversity or people of different racial or ethnic backgrounds within an organization. Nor is equality of outcomes necessary to achieve equity sufficient. There must also be an overt attempt to include others in all levels of the organization based on minority status and not on the ability to do the job.

DEI is directly opposed to meritocracy or moving ahead in an organization due to superior performance.[130] Eventually the organization will be damaged by this practice. If America continues to embrace DEI, I can't imagine how disastrous the results in the fields of medicine, finance, or especially our military will be.

## DEMOCRAT VS. REPUBLICAN: WHICH PARTY DOES "AMERICA" BEST?

For some time, the Democrat Party has been home to those who do not believe in American values and want to do everything possible to destroy our society. Though there are everyday American citizens who might be Democrats who hold the United States in high regard, the Democrat elected officials at the state and federal level do not. Author Michael Scheuer writes that the Democrats are the party of slavery, secession, segregation, and socialism.[131]

From the Civil War to the late 1960s, the Democrat Party has been the political party which oppressed Blacks in America and did everything it could to stop the Civil Rights movement. More recently they are the home of Socialists/Marxists who attack and oppress those who believe in American values. President Obama, a Democrat, made this intention clear when he stated that his purpose was to "fundamentally transform the United States of America"[132] during his administration. America does not need a fundamental transformation.

Comparing Democrat actions and Republican actions even briefly from the Civil War to today, a consistent pattern of Democrat oppression of Blacks emerges.

## Rs vs. Ds

The Democrats fought to expand slavery while the Republican Party was founded in 1854 as the anti-slavery party.[133]

The Republicans passed the Civil Rights Act of 1866 and the Reconstruction Act of 1867 to establish a new government system that would be fair to Blacks in the Democrat-controlled South.[134] In 1866 the Ku Klux Klan (KKK) began when Democrat and Confederate General Nathan Bedford became the first Grand Wizard in 1867.[135] Democrats fought to keep Blacks in slavery and away from the polls, and used the KKK to terrorize.[136]

In 1892, when the Democrats regained control of Congress they passed the Repeal Act of 1894 that overturned civil rights laws enacted by Republicans.[137]

Immediately when he took office in 1913, President Woodrow Wilson, a Democrat, reintroduced segregation in the federal government.[138]

Democrat President Franklin D. Roosevelt chose Harry Truman to be his vice president in 1944 after Truman had joined the Ku Klux Klan in Kansas City in 1922.[139]

George Wallace, Alabama's Democrat Governor, while standing in front of a school house shouted, "Segregation now, segregation tomorrow, segregation forever" in 1963.[140]

The Democrats voted against the Voting Rights Act of 1964. It was passed by the Republicans.[141]

In 1984 Virginia Democrat Governor Ralph Northam appeared in a photo on a page of his medical school yearbook in either blackface or KKK robes.[142]

When Democrat Senator Robert Byrd died on June 28, 2010, he was the highest ranking member of the Democrat Party, and he had been a leader in the KKK.[143]

After Black Republican Senator Tim Scott, in 2020, worked tirelessly on the Just and Unifying Solutions To Invigorate Communities Everywhere, or JUSTICE Act, to bring about reforms to the criminal justice system, Democrat Speaker of the House Nancy Pelosi disregarded his work, and the Senate Minority Whip, Dick Durbin, called the effort a "Token."[144]

---

With Democrat elected officials governing, it is clear why today in the U.S. we have extremely high energy prices, rampant inflation, increased racial strife (which started increasing during Obama's Presidency[145]), abandonment of the rule of law in Democrat-controlled cities leading to high crime rates, and elected Democrat officials governing against the will of the American people because they do not care about the American people. They only care about power. They need to maintain their power to further their agenda. They care about destroying the United States and imposing socialist rule.

# AMERICAN VALUES: ANOTHER VOICE

This country finds itself in the current downward social spiral due to the lack of elected officials governing according to American values. This anti-American stance is especially true of the Democrat officials who continue to follow the oppressive policies the Democrat Party has championed since the end of the Civil War. To govern, they embrace Socialism and use the principles of Marxism, which are counter to American values. The United States was built on the foundation of doing the right thing because liberty and virtue are two of our foundational values that have guided the country from our beginning up until now when a disturbing number of our institutions, the media, and the corporate world, which were generally more apolitical in the past, have decided to move left. We need to recommit to American values.

# 9

# THE INSTRUCTION MANUAL OF PERSONAL EXPERIENCE

*"In wisdom gathered over time I have found that every experience is a form of exploration."*

—**Ansel Adams,** Landscape Photographer

*"You gain strength, courage, and confidence by every experience in which you really stop to look fear in the face."*

—**Eleanor Roosevelt,** First Lady of the United States, 1933 - 1945

Growing up both in the United States and in foreign countries helped form my views. My wide range of experiences allowed me to encounter people of various cultures, ethnic backgrounds, religions, and economic levels. Many of the countries I spent time in also had vastly different political systems from America.

It was interesting to see how Queen Elizabeth II was revered in so many places far from England. As a stamp collector, I was amazed at how many countries had her portrait on their stamps. In school, I eventually learned that this came from the vast reaches of the British Empire around the world. Once I knew this history, I found it significant that though Britain was ruled by a constitutional monarchy, several of these countries also had one regime rule or a strong man who remained in power for many years—in many cases through a dictatorship. Observing these other forms of government at an early age caused me to think more about how the United States was governed.

In America itself, I witnessed or participated in experiences that touched on controversial issues such as racism and considering police officers as biased against Blacks or other minorities. This chapter is a collection of stories from my life that contribute to how I assess our current American culture, and formulated my responses to some of the criticism lobbed against the traditional values for which I advocate.

I was born in Norfolk, Virginia, on 5 December 1955 to Walter A. Grady Sr. and Dorothy H. Grady. With my older sister, Walteen P. Grady, arriving in the world in Houston, Texas, four years earlier, I was the baby for a while at least. Though my parents both grew up poor, by the time my sister was born we were a lower middle-class family. My father was employed as a vocational education professor at Virginia State College in Norfolk.

Before I was two years old, our family moved to Philadelphia, Pennsylvania, which as far as living in the United States is concerned, I call home. The move was a logical one because it placed us closer to my Uncle Gordon's family, who also lived in Philadelphia. Uncle Gordon was the primary caretaker for my grandmother, Viola Grady. Our family moving into the area provided an additional set of hands to help care for her. This was the setting where I grew up, and these were the key people who helped me grow and develop. My childhood dream was to become a pilot, and I was blessed to realize my dream. That dream focused my efforts in life. My desire turned into specific plans. The self-discipline that eventually enabled me to reach my goal is something I developed in my childhood and young adult years.

## Seeing the World Through a Young Boy's Eyes

### Lagos

When I was seven years old, my father was sent to Lagos, Nigeria, for a position working for the International Labor Organization (ILO). I remember looking down at the vastness of the Sahara Desert as we flew over Northern Africa during the final leg of our trip. Arriving at our destination, I immediately realized that Lagos was a very hot and muggy place.

Getting to know my new home, I found that many of the plants and wildlife were unfamiliar. I especially liked the palm trees. Nigeria has oil palms, so the nectar was harvested by the palm tree man. He would climb the tree with a lanyard made from a vine, reach the bottle that he had inserted the week before into the top or crown of the tree where the palm fronds or leaves attached, and replace it. He was harvesting a liquid from the tree that he would use to make palm wine. Another observation totally foreign to me previously was watching various lizards run up and down the walls of our third story apartment.

On one side of the yard that separated two wings of the apartment building compound was a banana grove. I was surprised to find out that bananas grow on a stem that can have more than 200 bananas on it. Seeing them in the grocery store, especially in the United States, did not give me any idea of how bananas grow.

Another benefit, besides getting firsthand knowledge about the world is that I made friends with children whose parents' various jobs had brought them to Lagos, also. I met peers from Sweden, Canada, Finland, and England. We had a great time running around outside in what was a child's paradise.

Unfortunately, there were two downsides to consider about my Lagos experiences. Warned about snakes, we stayed away from them if we saw any. Lagos has some very deadly snakes, like the Carpet Viper, the Black Spitting Cobra, and the Puff Adder. If I saw anything slithering in the weeds, I ran in the opposite direction.

I wish I could say I had no problem with any other animal in Lagos, but I can't. For some reason, dogs were attracted to me. Unfortunately, some of them bit me. By the time I left Nigeria I had endured three series of seven rabies shots. Back then, the shots were given in the stomach.

Since my mother was an RN and because of the nature of health care in Lagos at the time, my mother gave me the shots, twenty-one of them in the stomach. Believe me they were not my favorite due to the excruciating pain of the very thick serum being forced into my body. I almost feel the pain just thinking about it!

Regarding education, before I attended an American school in Lagos, which started during my last year there, I attended a British school. This school was much different than what I was familiar with from initially attending kindergarten through second grade in Philadelphia, Pennsylvania. Just about all the students in my class were Nigerian. We all wore school uniforms. My final year in Lagos, though, attending the American School, classroom activities were more normal as we celebrated U.S. holidays and sang familiar songs.

In the British school, desktops had inkwells in their upper parts in front of the hinges that allowed us to open the top and place our books inside the desk. Other things I remember are that 1066 was the Battle of Hastings, the beginning of England becoming a nation, and one of the Nigerian boys in my class reciting his thirteen times tables. We all had to recite up to our twelve times tables, but he went over and above this requirement. I also developed a British accent.

One very interesting trip my family took that I distinctly remember was visiting Dahomey, or Benin, which borders Nigeria to the west. Slaves were gathered here from the interior of Africa and placed on slave ships bound for various places including America. I remember seeing a small one-room building with chains with manacles attached to the walls. These were obviously used for restraining the slaves until they were put on ships.

My mind visualized eerie thoughts of what it must have been like as a captive from African tribal warfare and then soon to become a slave. This was sobering.

## Home to Philadelphia

After living in Nigeria, we returned to Philadelphia where I once again attend Pennell Elementary School. After a very short time I realized that having a British accent in a Philadelphia Inner City Public School was not cool…not cool at all! So I very quickly lost it!

I progressed through fifth and half of sixth grade at Pennell. The teachers were strict and did not allow any foolishness in the classroom. However, it was very clear they cared about us and wanted each of us to do well.

I remember one day in fifth grade our teacher was so dissatisfied with the behavior of every student in the classroom she had us form a circle around her with one of our hands extended out, palm facing up. Then, she walked by each student and struck the palm of the hand with the flat side of a ruler. Some students were whacked once. Some of us, more than once…but everyone was whacked. When we sat down, we all behaved.

In sixth grade, I remember an incident where a student made the mistake of pulling out his .38 Caliber pistol and was showing it to the boy next to him while the teacher was teaching. She stopped speaking, walked smartly over to him, grabbed the gun in one hand, his ear in the other hand, stood him up and walked him out of the classroom. She was much shorter than he was, so I vividly remember her reaching up over her head to hang on to his ear. She returned in about ten minutes, and we did not see that young man in our class ever again. This incident happened during the late sixties, when Philadelphia had a serious street gang problem.

## Bangkok

After a while, my dad applied for and was hired by the United States Agency for International Development (USAID), and the agency sent him to Vietnam. Because of the war, the family was safe havened in Bangkok, Thailand. It was there that I attended the International School of Bangkok (ISB), where I completed sixth grade and eventually graduated from high school. Our family spent six and a half years in Bangkok.

## AMERICAN VALUES: ANOTHER VOICE

Though very hot and humid, the landscape in Thailand was beautiful. Even more noteworthy was the unique "Thai food", especially the fruit. The pineapple, mango, and papaya were delicious. (An aside: Many years later while living in Korea when the U.S. Air Force stationed me there, I had the opportunity to take my bride on a vacation. One of the places we visited was Bangkok, Thailand. Donna remarked that the papaya in Thailand was the most delicious papaya that she had ever tasted. I agree.

Thailand also had dangerous wildlife, but since I'd lived in Africa, this did not capture my attention. Some of the poisonous snakes include the King Cobra, Siamese Spitting Cobra, Banded Krait, Green Keelback, and the Russel's Siamese Viper. Though elephants are not overtly dangerous, people do need to be careful around them. I enjoyed riding one during the Thai Elephant Round-up in Surin Province, located in Northeastern, Thailand. I daydreamed I was Hannibal crossing the Alps into Italy to engage the Romans in battle. But then the very warm temperatures and humidity of Thailand brought me back to reality.

I lived in Thailand from 1967 to 1973, and during that period the Vietnam War reached its peak in personnel and then began to decline as the U.S. struggled to drawdown and end the conflict. The size of the student body at ISB reflected this. When I first arrived, classrooms were quite packed with students. By the time I graduated, the classrooms had many unoccupied seats.

About half of the students were Americans, the other half came from all over the world. The parents of the children mainly consisted of military or business people, diplomats, or missionaries. The children of a few of the school faculty also attended the school. We had a very diverse group. Notably absent from the student body were native born Thai citizens although we did have a few Thai students who had passports foreign to Thailand due to a parent not being a Thai citizen. The Thai government prevented Thai citizens from attending the school because they wanted the students to be taught in the Thai language.

ISB was an excellent school. The curriculum was academically challenging and there was a wide range of activities, such as sports, science and service clubs, and theater to take part in. Though I was on the track, soccer, and volleyball teams, I was also involved in student government all four years of high school. I served on the Student Supreme Court my freshman year and was elected Sophomore, Junior, and Senior Class President. I thoroughly enjoyed serving my fellow schoolmates.

## Encountering Racism

Traveling overseas during my formative years, I was not only the only American in most situations, but I was most often the only Black American. This was not something that I really thought much about, especially in my preteen years. Depending on where I was, many children from other cultures would come up to me and touch my hair to see what it felt like, or they would place their arm next to mine to compare skin color. However, other friends who weren't Black also had similar experiences, especially people who were blonde.

Since that was the environment we grew up in, we grew accustomed to being treated as an oddity. However, Thailand was where I experienced my first instances of overt racial discrimination. I was living there in the late sixties and early seventies, during the aftermath of the severe racial riots in Detroit, and after the assassination of Dr. Martin Luther King Jr.

In general, Thailand and our school were very calm in that respect, but we all knew what was going on back in the U.S. The calmness was largely attributed to most Americans representing the U.S. either in a military, diplomatic, or business position. We were very aware that in some cases if children caused trouble in the community, the family would be deported back to the United States. Being deported was not good.

In addition, the American Ambassador to Thailand, Mr. Leonard Unger, whose son was my classmate, set the tone for the community. I heard the tail end of a conversation my mother was having with one of her friends one day when she mentioned, "Mr. Unger wouldn't put up with that." I was not sure what 'that' was, but it was very clear that he had the respect of all the Americans in Bangkok. And this is as it should be. One of the Ambassador's responsibilities is to maintain good relations by making sure that the American community continues to make a favorable impression on the people of the host country.

My very first racism experience happened one day when I visited my friend Paul Fueling at his house. We decided to go swimming since it was a very hot afternoon, typical in Bangkok. The landlord who rented the house to the Fuelings also owned another property down the street that had a pool in the back yard. The landlord had given permission for the Fuelings to swim in the pool, so Paul and I went over to the house and swam.

After about an hour, we saw the landlord's wife showing a family around the house. It was vacant at the time. After she noticed us in the pool, she came over and whispered in Paul's ear. He looked at her rather strangely, then came over and let me know that we needed to leave. He didn't comment. We went back to his house, where I stayed for a few more hours and then I went home.

Later that night my mom received a telephone call from Mrs. Fueling. After they talked for a while and she hung up, she came over to me and let me know that Mrs. Fueling would be coming over to talk with me.

Once she arrived Mrs. Fueling explained to me that the reason her son and I left the pool earlier that day was because the landlord's wife was showing the empty house to an American family who happened to be White and might possibly rent it. The landlord's wife had been afraid that if they saw me in the pool, they might not have wanted to rent the house.

Mrs. Fueling further explained that the landlord's wife had been very apologetic when she came over to make an explanation, but Mrs. Fueling still thought she needed to let me know what went on and why. She was very unhappy this happened to her son and me and thought that it was important for me to know that she was sad it happened, and this kind of thinking was not acceptable as far as she was concerned.

My mom, Mrs. Fueling, and I ended up having a good general discussion about race and what was occurring in the United States.

Though there were other incidents that occurred because of my skin color, the next overt event happened right after I graduated from high school but before I left for college. One of my close friends in high school was Joe Lampe. His father was a Naval Chaplain. Unfortunately, Joe's father was assigned to Hong Kong at the end of our junior year, so he left ISB and spent his senior year in Hong Kong. For a graduation present, my parents bought me a ticket to visit Joe in Hong Kong, who would be graduating a week after we did.

We had a great time. Hong Kong was an exciting city. During my stay Joe took me to a party. While there, I ran into my seventh-grade math teacher. She had moved to teach in Hong Kong several years earlier after her husband was transferred there by his company. When she saw me, she smiled, and we had a very pleasant conversation. Finally, she asked me where I was going to attend college. When I told her about the Air Force Academy, she showed great surprise with wide eyes and her mouth gaping open that turned into a very broad smile.

You need to understand that my brain didn't wake up until eighth grade, when I began to show signs of academic life, and started doing well in my subjects and excelling in math and science. I was definitely not one of her better students the year before. She was so excited that she immediately pulled me over to her husband and exclaimed, "Tony was in my math class in seventh grade, and he's going to the Air Force Academy for college!"

Her husband was much less enthusiastic. He looked at me from head to toe for a moment, wasn't smiling, and looked down his nose at me asking, "How did you get in there?"

My mother and sister can attest to the fact that I by no means have any low self-esteem issues. Without batting an eye, I looked at him and said, "I applied like everybody else and was selected." When I returned home to Bangkok a few days later, I relayed the story to my mother. She chuckled and discussed with me various reasons connected to my race that might explain why he made his condescending comment.

My next worrisome race-related incident occurred at the end of the first six weeks of training (known as "Beast") at the Air Force Academy. But, before I get to the details of the incident, I first need to set the stage. A week after graduation from the International School of Bangkok, I arrived in Colorado Springs where the Air Force Academy is located, and spent my last night as a free man in a hotel.

## AMERICAN VALUES: ANOTHER VOICE

The next morning, I met Scott Hutt, who was also headed to the Academy. We waited for the bus to take us to the cadet area. We were classmates, and both made the Academy Track & Field Team. We became lifelong friends. But, prior to all that we had to suffer through, I mean survive Basic Cadet Training, BCT, or more affectionately called Beast.

This ordeal lasted six weeks. Once we were in-processed, the Academy dubbed us Basic Cadets or just Basics. Our training cadre were upperclassman who were Juniors referred to as Two-Degrees (2°), and seniors referred to as One-Degrees (1°) or Firsties. There were approximately 1,500[146] new Basic Cadets. They divided us into ten squadrons with approximately 150 Basic Cadets in each squadron. Within each squadron, we were further divided into four flights, each consisting of about 40 Basics. And the flights were made up of three elements each consisting of ten Basics.

The upperclassman filled the staff position in each squadron and trained us. Each squadron was supervised by a Commissioned Officer, usually a Captain or Major. They stayed in the background. Most of them were Air Force officers, but there was an occasional officer from another U.S. military service branch like the Army who might also fill this position. They were called an AOC or Air Officer Commanding. These officers made sure things didn't get too far out of hand, most of the time. Over the six-weeks the Academy upperclassmen transitioned us from cocky high schoolers into a cohesive team capable of receiving orders and carrying them out. We were in very good shape after six weeks, doing all our favorite calisthenics like push-ups, pullups, and running in the rarefied Colorado air at an elevation of 7,258 feet above sea level.

Because of the nature of the training system, Basic Cadets only became familiar with the members of their element and their flight. A Basic did not interact with the other flights in the squadron or with anyone in any of the other squadrons. They were distant.

After completing Beast, each flight of 40 basic cadets, now referred to as Cadets Fourth Class, would go into a different academic squadron, numbered one through forty. This is where the now Cadet Fourth Class would spend the first year at the Academy, and it is at this juncture I encountered the issue of race.

The day before we were to enter our academic squadrons, my flight commander, who was the junior in charge of my flight, came into my room, sat me down, and said, "Tomorrow your flight is going to become part of Cadet Squadron 6. However, you will not be going with them. You are going to go with the flight that is entering Cadet Squadron 29. The Academy has a policy[147] that Blacks cannot go into a squadron by themselves at the end of Basic Cadet Training. They must enter the academic squadron in a group of two or three."

Of course, I didn't say anything, but his comments hit me like a ton of bricks. I was leaving the other thirty-nine guys that I'd gotten to know over the last six weeks and bonded with as I started my academic year. That was no small issue.

It is beyond the scope of this book to explain why this was so alarming, but it is sufficient to say that during that first year the freshmen, fourth classmen, or doolies as affectionally called, in each academic squadron had to depend on each other and cover each other's backs. If not, the upperclassmen would devour all of them. So, now I had to get to know a totally different group of guys right when things were going to get busy with going to class, running track, and all the other activities I would become involved in during that first year.

I didn't need this added stress. The Academy did not want any Black cadet to feel isolated. Though the thought behind this policy might have been noble, it missed a glaring major point. The purpose of Beast was to forge a team. After that team was formed, removing a member of the team was detrimental to the end objective.

This change of squadron and some other things that happened indicated to me that some at the Academy did not know I was Black until I arrived.

Another incident the following year was much more subtle and yet complex. During my sophomore, or Three-Degree (3°), year at the Air Force Academy I was taking political science, one of the core curriculum courses. After taking a few quizzes in the class I realized I wasn't receiving very good grades.

I also noticed that when I would raise my hand in class to answer a question, the instructor never called on me; he always called on another cadet. Something truly odd was happening because even when he would ask a question and I was the only one with my hand up, he would ignore me and just answer the question himself. Then we were given a major test referred to as a Graded Review, or GR, and I failed it.

Now I was really concerned.

If this had been an economics class, maybe there was a chance that I might perform poorly since I was more wired for engineering and math courses as opposed to what we cadets called "fuzzy studies." However, having spent my life traveling all over the world and seeing first-hand how a country uses its instruments of power to further its national interests, I understood political science.

Needing to share my worries about the class, I made an appointment to see my squadron Air Officer Commanding (AOC), Capt. James C. Lesseig. He was an Air Force officer who had flown the McDonald Douglas F-4 Phantom in Vietnam before coming to the Academy. He was quite reserved, but exacting.

During our meeting I relayed to him what was happening in political science and he said that he would investigate it. The next day he called me into his office and told me that instead of going to political science the next day, I should report to the office of the Course Director of the Political Science course I was taking.

The next day wearing my dress uniform consisting of a jacket with my insignia displaying my rank, my name tag above my right breast pocket, my singular National Defense ribbon on my left breast pocket, and below, in the middle of the pocket, a silver wreath signifying that I was on the Commandant's List[148], I walked in and saluted smartly and said, "Sir, Cadet Third Class Grady reporting as ordered!"

Behind the desk sat an Air Force Major similarly dressed but in Air Force blues with pilot wings and rows of ribbons on his left breast. He returned my salute and said, "At ease Mr. Grady, please have a seat."

It was LUCKY Ekman! Major Leonard Ekman was a Vietnam war hero. During the Vietnam War he flew the Republic F-105 Thunderchief, affectionately called the Thud, because of the poor glide characteristics when this airplane's single engine quit. The direction of the flight after this unfortunate event was straight down to the ground.

During his first tour in Vietnam, he was shot down on his 131st mission. During his second tour, he flew the F-105 on the Wild

Weasel mission where pilots would intentionally fly in a way to have the enemy's Surface-to-Air Missile or SAM radars lock on to them and prepare to shoot them down. However, before that happened, the awesome aircraft would shoot an air-to-ground missile, known as the HARM or Highspeed Anti-Radiation Missile, to seek out and destroy the SAM launch site on the ground. This was a challenging and very dangerous mission.

I was awestruck to say the least.

I should note here that one important characteristic of the Air Force Academy was that cadets were taught by officers who had done what they hoped to do, namely become an Air Force pilot. There was a program called AM-370, or Airmanship 370, where once a semester cadets had the opportunity to, instead of attending morning or afternoon classes, a small group of cadets at a time were bussed to Peterson Field, now Peterson Air Force Base, in Colorado Springs. After arriving at the airfield, the cadets would fly in the backseat of a Lockheed T-33 Shooting Star, for which the pilot was an Academy faculty member.

Major Ekman began the conversation and asked me several questions. We talked for about an hour. There was a short stack of 8 ½" X 11" papers stapled together resting in front of him on the desk. At the end of the conversation, he turned the stapled papers over, and it was my Graded Review on which I had not performed very well.

As he looked at me, he said, "Mr. Grady, if you had turned this GR in to me for a grade, I'd have failed you also." He paused for a moment, and I was horrified. He then cracked a smile, changing his expression, and said, "But during our conversation I have tested your knowledge of the political science subject matter, and you have a very good grasp of the concepts that we're teaching. You should not be doing as poorly in the class as your scores are reflecting. So, I'm going to move you to another section where you will have a different instructor."

I was relieved. He dismissed me, and I stood and exchanged salutes with Major Ekman and left his office. The next political science class I attended was in another room. My grades greatly improved, and I did quite well in the class.

If this were all that one had to consider about my inability to connect with my first political science instructor, it might not seem that there was a racial component at the heart of the story. However, when I shared with some fellow cadets about my experience in the class, I discovered that another cadet friend of mine who had the same instructor but was in a class that met at a different time was having the same experience. He also happened to be Black.

When I discussed with him the steps I was taking, he chose not to speak to his Air Officer Commanding and told me he just needed to work harder. He failed the class at the end of the semester.

One point about failing classes at the Air Force Academy is that failing happens, but it is rare. Though the curriculum is challenging, it is almost as difficult to fail as it is to get the highest grade. Generally, there is some reason that a cadet fails. This friend of mine was not someone who would fail a class. So, when I reflect on the matter, it appears to me that this instructor may have had a problem. I will never really know.

The final incident I include here occurred after I graduated from pilot training and reported to Carswell Air Force Base in Fort Worth, Texas, for my first operational assignment. I was going through upgrade training to become a Boeing B-52D Heavy Bomber Co-pilot.

One Saturday afternoon some of the other pilots from my class and I met off the Air Force Base at a McDonalds to have lunch. After lunch we talked for a while then I was the first one to leave.

On Monday before class started, the classmates who had joined me for lunch came up to me and said, "We need to tell you what happened after you left McDonalds."

I was wondering what could have happened because everything seemed fine when I left the restaurant. They went on saying, "An older gentleman approached us and asked, 'Who are you boys, and what are you doing here?' We responded that we are Second Lieutenant Air Force Pilots attending B-52 upgrade training at Carswell Air Force Base." They then told me that the man paused for a moment and then asked, "And the Black fella who was with you, who is he?"

My classmates said, "He's also a Second Lieutenant Air Force Pilot in class with us." Then the man asked, "Are they smart enough to fly airplanes?" My classmates couldn't believe what they'd heard, and they thought I should know to be on guard for what I might find while I was out and about in the city.

As it turned out Fort Worth was a great city. I lived there three years and during that time I met my wife. However, I mentioned in the last chapter that I think most of my high school classmates who graduated from ISB experienced culture shock when they returned to the United States for college. This incident was part of the last bit of culture shock I experienced. This incident was very clearly racially motivated.

## Run-ins with the Police

I've received two speeding tickets. The first was during my senior year at the Academy, trying to make it from Colorado Springs to Denver airport on time to catch my airplane for Thanksgiving leave that year. I left after completing my last final, and my roommate, who was staying in Colorado Springs for the holiday break, agreed to drive my car back to the Academy from the airport.

We were on the outskirts of Denver almost to the airport, traveling at a rather high rate of speed, when an unmarked police car turned on its lights and pulled us over. The encounter was uneventful. I was given a ticket, and the policeman took pity on me and wrote it so I would not need to appear in court. That was a relief.

The Academy didn't like cadets receiving speeding tickets, and appearing in court would have been completely out of the question! If that happened, my car would probably have been impounded until I graduated. I dodged a bullet.

The next speeding ticket I received, while traveling along Interstate 10, was when I drove from Williams Air Force Base outside Phoenix, Arizona, to Carswell Air Force Base in Fort Worth, Texas. I'd just graduated from Undergraduate Pilot Training and was on my way to my first operational assignment.

As I drove along the road a few hours east of El Paso, Texas, I was startled by a police car with its lights flashing right next to mine with four policemen in it all pointing at me to pull over. As I looked at my speedometer the needle was decelerating through 110 mph. I realized at that moment that I'd fallen asleep, and one of the front wheels of my 1976 Datsun 280Z was in a groove in the road probably worn by semi-trucks which guided me straight down the highway.

The maneuver of the police vehicle woke me up.

After I pulled off to the side of the road, the Officer came over to my rolled down window and asked if I was on my way to an emergency. I said, "No Sir, but I think I'm about to have one."

He informed me that they had followed me for a while with their lights flashing before pulling alongside my car. Their action probably saved my life, or at least kept me from having a serious accident. He wrote me a citation for speeding, and because we were out in the middle of nowhere, I was instructed to follow him to the nearest town where I paid the ticket. Event over.

I mentioned receiving these tickets because neither of these encounters with law enforcement put my life in danger from the officers. At no time did I think they were harassing or threatening me because I was Black.

It is interesting to note there is some indication that Blacks and Hispanics are "fifty percent more likely to experience some form of force in interactions with police."[149] In the incidences of the police attempting to stop violent crimes, a Harvard study shows that "[B]lacks are less likely to be shot at first, if anything."[150]

A very small number of loudly vocal people assert that the police routinely "hunt" for minorities to inflict violence on them, but in my encounters, that was not the case at all.

I've shared my life up to this point in time, how I came to be a Nevadan, and what shaped my thinking process that informs my political viewpoint. I've described how I was blessed to have parents who loved me enough to raise me with solid values, American values.

Those values were reinforced by my grandmother and uncle and helped guide me as I was growing up, and since I grew up inside and outside the United States, I became very patriotic experiencing firsthand that I was born in the greatest country in the world. Though they were poor and grew up in the Jim Crow South governed by Democrat political office holders, the family members who shaped me as I grew up persevered and overcame the obstacles that were intentionally placed in front of them their entire lives.

Education was a key to their success, and I understood this reality from a very early age. God blessed me tremendously to have a life path filled with family members of such good character and with opportunities to learn about and better understand humanity. My purpose has been to honor God, take care of my family, and serve my country and community. If anything, my resolve to do that is stronger than ever.

# 10
## SO WHAT?

*"Happy are those who dream dreams  
and are ready to pay the price to make them come true."*

—**Leon J. Suenens,** *Archbishop of Mechelen-Brussels  
from 1961 to 1979.*

My answer to the chapter title question would be that my parents introduced me to the American Dream, and because of them I prospered, and because I prospered, I seek to help others do the same.

At least some part of my motivation also comes from three dramatic incidents seared into my memory by the realization of how close I came to not being here at all. Because God saw fit to keep me safe, my gratefulness draws me toward doing my part to protect others from what I see are enemies of Truth and Virtue in the world, and particularly in America.

I offer three near-death narratives, and then my assessment of several current world affairs before I end on my suggested solutions to certain serious problems we are currently facing in the United States.

## NOT MY DAY TO DIE

## PART 1

Though I was born in Norfolk, Virginia, my earliest childhood memory took place in Philadelphia, Pennsylvania, when I stepped from the curb onto the street in front of our apartment building right before I was hit by a truck.

I remember stepping off the curb.

I do not remember being hit.

I was only three years old at the time, and survived because the truck rolled over me and my body passed between the tires. The driver did not even know he hit me because I was so small that he probably could not see me as he looked out over the hood of his truck.

When he found out later what happened after someone told him, he came by the house and humbly apologized to my mother. Fortunately, my collarbone was the only part of my body that was broken. However, if you ask my sister, I'm not sure she would agree that was the only place I suffered damage because of this accident...

My father was in Indonesia at the time, and my mother just returned home from working in the hospital that day. I imagine she quickly returned there with me. This is the first of the three major near-death incidents I remember.

## PART 2

The second incident occurred when I was eight while we were living in Lagos, Nigeria, when my parents and I visited a dock on the lagoon in Lagos harbor. We were probably touring the city. I walked out onto a cement dock with steps leading down to the lagoon. I wanted to get closer to the water to see what was below the surface.

The bottom step of the dock was covered with a thin puddle of water that had washed up onto it. The water was stagnant and probably remained there from when the lagoon water level was slightly higher, and had covered the step.

I didn't really think much about the green mass that was also under the water on the step, so I stepped down on it. Instantly I was flat on my back looking up at the sky! My clothes were soaked down my back.

I looked around and didn't see my parents. Fear shot through me as it occurred to me that they hadn't noticed my fall. Right next to my shoulder was the deep dark murky water of the lagoon that I'm pretty sure was much deeper than I was tall. I somehow had to get on my feet again without flipping into that water. I knew if that happened I would drown because at that time in my life I couldn't swim.

With the back of my shirt drenched in icky green wetness, I carefully rolled over, grabbed the dry upper step, and used my knee to pull my body back up onto the dry part of the dock. It was only when I saw my father and knew he saw me that I felt safe instead of terrified.

## PART 3

The third time I saw my life pass in front of me was near the end of United States Air Force Undergraduate Pilot Training. Two student crews were learning how to fly tactical formation, which required two jets to fly abeam. Our two Northrop T-38 Talons, the Air Force's advanced supersonic training aircraft, were flying line abreast, with a mile in between separating us.

Leading this maneuver, I signaled my wingman, who was my roommate and good friend from the Air Force Academy, John Graper, to rejoin on my wing. In rejoining he turned and flew toward my airplane, decreasing the mile of separation between us to position his aircraft in the fingertip position, about three feet wingtip separation.

When we'd briefed this maneuver before the flight, we'd agreed that this rejoin would be to the number three position, simulating that there were four airplanes in the formation instead of just two of us. This simulation meant that even though John's initial position in the tactical formation was one mile off my right wing, when he rejoined, he would move his airplane to the fingertip position on my left wing. That was the plan, anyway.

But then John slightly overshot, or went a little too far behind my airplane and a few feet higher in altitude, causing him to lose sight of me. In a fraction of a second, he was directly above my airplane and descending on top of me.

When I saw the rivets on the bottom of his airplane, I pushed my airplane over rapidly by moving the control stick forward as fast as I could! My instructor was immediately pinned up against the canopy in the backseat of the jet because of the negative Gs created by our rapid dive toward the ground. Meanwhile, John's instructor had taken control of their airplane and pulled them straight up away from us.

Despite the adrenaline rush caused by the extremely dangerous potential crash, because our formation was initially flying at about 20,000 feet above the ground, we had plenty of room to maneuver to avoid each other. Of course, we did have to make the right moves in time, and we had.

When things settled down, there were some choice communications over the radio, and I noticed the G-meter displayed I had put negative four Gs on the airplane. This reading means we felt like we were floating upwards four times greater than the force of gravity pulls objects towards the ground. So, instead of being pulled toward the ground, we were being pushed toward the sky.

The T-38 Talon is only rated for a maximum of negative 2.9 Gs[151], so the instructor took control of the airplane and gingerly flew it back to the airfield just in case something was damaged causing the aircraft to fly abnormally. All went well and we landed uneventfully.

After the debrief, John and I met back at our rooms, which were joined by a kitchen, located in the Bachelor Officers Quarters on Williams Air Force Base, and we both experienced the aftereffects of our close call. When we looked at each other in the eye, both of us began to shake uncontrollably for a few seconds as we realized that we had had a very close brush with death.

We sat down and discussed the incident for a few hours until we had a bit of closure. John had taken it extremely hard because since he was rejoining in close formation next to my airplane, he felt it was his actions that put all four of our lives in danger.

Though I had many other similar close calls later in life, especially while flying in the Air Force, they did not affect me as much. Perhaps because I had more confidence or stronger faith, they did not make the same impression on me as these first three instances.

---

I consider my life a gift from God who has protected me through the many instances that threatened to end it. Realizing God spared me, I daily seek to live with a purpose. This commitment is a reason I continue a life of service.

I care about people, especially those who are from the United States of America, so I have formulated a few responses that might lead to solving some of the problems facing the nation today. As a free and united people, we can think through our problems, develop, and put in place solutions to end our downward spiral. Solving these problems will give our children, grandchildren, and all those who come after us the chance for a future that continues to offer the freedoms and safety America once stood for as a beacon on the hill.[152]

## CURRENT WORLD SITUATION

In the last four years, the world has become a much more dangerous place. Regional instability has increased causing countries to realign to protect their national interests. Protecting interests is normal, but U.S. actions and rhetoric are causing other countries uncertainty in how to effectively regain stability.

This uncertainty has come about due to missteps made by the United States, which damaged national interests. The decreasing role of the U.S. serving as a respected world leader is one of the missteps. Other countries are losing confidence in the ability of the United States to effectively help them. Vastly different worldviews between recent U.S. presidential administrations have caused an ineffective use of the country's national instruments of power, through which it engages other countries in the world. U.S. actions on the world stage are now inconsistent.

By examining how three categories, or national instruments, of power—diplomatic, military, and economic—have not been used well of late, I will briefly touch on why the relationships between countries around the world are becoming less stable. U.S. missteps, decreasing support of long-held American objectives, and a decrease in U.S. military power offer insight into the state of the world today.

The Afghanistan withdrawal was a glaring misstep. This was the longest war in U.S. history beginning in September 2001 and ending in August 2021.[153] Unclear objectives cause wars to drag on, as this one did for twenty years. However, the final actions in Afghanistan resulted from poor military planning along with a significant diplomatic inconsistency between two presidential administrations. The poor planning resulted in billions of dollars in military equipment being left in the hands of the Taliban, who swiftly took over as the United States withdrew.[154] Also, due to confusion, as many as 14,000 Americans were left behind.[155]

These actions do not encourage those from whom the United States might seek assistance to conduct military operations in the future. This scenario is likely to happen because of the rise of new alliances, such as these identified by Shoshana Bryen, Senior Director of The Jewish Policy Center and Editor of *inFOCUS Quarterly*:

*"China-Saudi Arabia, China-Iran, Israel-China, Tesla-China, China-Democratic Republic of Congo (DRC), Brazil/Venezuela/Cuba-China. Saudi Arabia-Syria, Saudi Arabia-Israel, Iran-Saudi Arabia, Saudi Arabia-Palestinian Authority, Iran-Iraq, Russia-Iran, Iran-Venezuela/Cuba/Nicaragua, Russia-Israel, Japan-South Korea, Japan-Russia."*[156, 157]

Many of these alliances have come into being during the last four years due to U.S. missteps and its failure to act logically internationally.

Besides the Afghanistan withdrawal debacle already discussed, the United States is sending mixed signals to Taiwan through President Biden's repeated confusing comments over the One China policy.[158] China is threatening Taiwan because it considers the island a breakaway province and seeks to eventually bring it back under mainland government control.[159] The United States isn't dealing with China effectively, nor Taiwan.

Moreover, China is expanding its influence on the continent of Africa as part of its ongoing effort to overtake the United States in world dominance. Making great economic progress, China has gained access to Africa's abundant resources[160] such as diamonds, sugar, salt, gold, iron, cobalt, uranium, copper, bauxite, silver, petroleum, and natural gas. China's Belt and Road Initiative[161] uses diplomacy to greatly increase its ability to obtain strategic rare earth minerals from Africa.

That China is expanding its military reach by gaining a port in Equatorial Guinea where it could start to challenge the U.S. Navy in the Atlantic Ocean[162] is of great concern.

With regard to another Asian country, Japan, a U.S. ally, is in negotiations with Russia, a U.S. adversary, to supply it with oil.[163] This proposition directly conflicts with the oil sanctions that the United States put in place against Russia because it invaded Ukraine.[164]

Particularly worrisome are the significant changes in diplomatic agreements in the last three years brought on by perceived American weakness such as the realignment in the Middle East between Saudi Arabia and Iran. A significant decrease in the number of ships make it unlikely that the U.S. Naval Fleet will be able to keep natural choke points like the Strait of Malacca and the Strait of Sunda open if a conflict occurs in the South Pacific.[165] The American 7th Fleet maintained free passage in this area of the world for many years.

During the Cold War, the Navy maintained 150 ships at sea but now has a goal of maintaining 75.[166] This decrease in Naval strength leaves merchant ships that conduct commerce throughout the world vulnerable to attack, which could significantly disrupt global supply chains. Also, a decrease in the ability to protect strategic sea lanes makes it much more difficult to have a strong and capable national defense.

Perhaps the most injurious result of these missteps characterized by the botched Afghanistan withdrawal is the unfavorable perception of our president held by other world leaders. Their actions, especially those of our adversaries, show that they see Mr. Biden as weak, lacking insight, and failing to live up to the reputation of the President of the United States as a strong and decisive commander in chief. Biden's weakness directly led to the invasion of Ukraine by Russia on February 24, 2022, and the barbaric attack by Hamas on Israel on October 7, 2023. His weakness also encouraged the Chinese to violate

U.S. airspace by sending a spy balloon over the heart our country from January 28 to February 4, 2023.

These few examples of U.S. missteps, diplomatic inconsistencies, and a poor use of the national instruments of power, already add up to a need for a change of direction. The United States is in decline as a world leader, and it has contributed and is contributing to the instability in diplomatic relations between countries.

## AMERICA IS IN TROUBLE AT HOME, TOO

Democrat Party leaders do not have a monopoly on racial prejudice determining their actions. However, Democrat Party policies formally put into action segregation, Black Codes, and the Jim Crow laws. They used oppression to maintain control. In contrast, the Republican Party began with the objective of ending slavery. The Republicans were the party that produced the Emancipation Proclamation, written by President Abraham Lincoln, freeing the slaves in the south.

There have been Democrat leaders who have benefited the country, such as John F. Kennedy, who cut taxes and made sure America was strong internationally, and Congressman Ike Skelton, who was a great supporter of a strong military. Congressman Skelton helped to create the Air Force's School of Advanced Air Power Studies (now Air Power and Space Studies), the Air Force's premier strategy school. Senator Sam Nunn, who was a moderate and foreign policy expert, worked tirelessly on minimizing the threat of nuclear weapons, especially encouraging the former Soviet Satellite Republics to dispose of their nuclear weapons as quickly as possible.[167] Senator Patrick Moynihan, who was a champion of helping families, worked to stabilize Social Security.[168] Not that long ago, Senator Joe Lieberman worked to strengthen America's national security and national defense. Most importantly, Senator Lieberman was a steady voice of reason in helping to bring opposing sides to useful solutions in the U.S. Senate.[169]

Today, the overwhelming majority of Democrat office holders and political leaders are leftists who champion the party's legacy of oppression. Their severely flawed worldview that there are only oppressors and the oppressed is the bankrupt theory of Karl Marx. Marxism subjects and enslaves the people of any country living under its form of government, eventually forcing them to live in abject poverty.

I would put what is happening at our Southern border at the top of the list of Democrat policies harming America. By failing to operate our borders as they should be operated, the Democrats are willfully creating a new underclass by allowing masses of people to enter the country illegally. Democrat leaders are failing in their constitutional responsibility to protect the integrity of our borders as stated in Article IV, Section 4 of the U.S. Constitution. But then they have no regard for the Constitution of the United States[170] that has served well to protect individual freedoms for over two centuries.

A huge percentage of the people entering the county illegally do not arrive with the financial ability to support themselves. Because of this, the government uses American taxpayer money to subsidize them. Many who come in are gang members who have no intention of following U.S. laws, and many who are brought here by gangs are being sex-trafficked.

Another type of trafficking attached to illegal border crossings has to do with drugs. Many in the drug-trafficking group are controlled by the Mexican Drug Cartels. America has seen a steep increase in the entry of illegal drugs, especially fentanyl, which originates in China, and which is the number one cause of death of people between the ages of 18 to 45.[171]

Illegal immigration creates serious problems for America's children. Childhood diseases that were eradicated in the U.S. are coming back because persons entering illegally are infected with them, like Polio[172] and Tuberculosis (TB).[173] Also, many schools in the cities that are receiving those entering illegally were not designed for large numbers of young students who do not speak English, our national language. Knowing our language is very important because to be successful in the United States a person must be able to speak and understand English.

The invasion of people illegally entering the country results in financial, medical, and social burdens, but the current Democrat office holders at the national level have shown they do not care. Those entering the country illegally are not initially entering their cities, as noted in Martha's Vineyard, a place where many of the elites in U.S. society live. The people transported there who had entered the country illegally were removed very swiftly, within twenty-four hours.[174]

The outrageous hypocrisy of the outcome brought by Democrat-established "open borders," is that the most vulnerable of our society, struggling families many of whom are minorities, end up the most detrimentally impacted because illegals take away jobs and overload medical care facilities in low-income areas. The very demographic the Democrats claim they represent and fight for is the demographic suffering greatest harm from the policies of current Democrat elected officials.

The second major problem Democrats in Washington have to take the blame for is America's economic decline. Under the current Democrat leadership, the U.S. government is finding more and more ways to tax the American people. Also, they are appropriating and authorizing funding in a way that is not in line with the originally established process for accomplishing this important function. The government is printing more and more money with nothing of value to support it. The Gross Domestic Product (GDP) is barely growing[175], and the national debt has exceeded an alarming 34 trillion dollars.

When the government spends money it doesn't have, money loses value, and when a currency loses value, that's called inflation. As noted in the previous paragraph, the U.S. government can print money at will, which contributes to increasing inflation.

The high price of energy also feeds inflation. Costly energy is a direct result of the current President's policies and administration that intentionally restrict the supply of the most inexpensive form of energy available for use today, which is oil, artificially causing the price to rise.

When the cost of energy rises it causes the price of everything else to increase because energy is a basic link in the global supply chain. Everything manufactured or grown requires energy. Every item in the store is transported using energy. Therefore, the higher cost of energy results in a cost-of-living increase.

Many wealthy Democrat office holders are effectively insulated from the very inflation their actions are inflicting on our country. Rising inflation decreases the number of items hard-working Americans can buy with the money they earn to the point that such large increases in the prices of everything sometimes force the poorest among us to choose between eating and paying their heating bill.[176]

America was not this way in the twenty-first century until recently, and this is not the way it should be. During the Covid-19 Pandemic the draconian government measures forced on the people did not help to lessen the spread of the virus, and Democrat-sponsored government collusion with social media censored anyone who pointed out this fact. Much of the information regarding Covid-19 coming out today shows these useless measures were detrimental to decreasing the spread of the disease.[177]

Regardless of what people and much of the leftist mainstream media say, the evidence shows that the Democrat party continues to be the anti-democracy party of oppression and is driving America into the ground.

## THE FIX STARTS HERE:

The American people should not accept any of this detrimental way of governing. The United States is in this position because we have poor leaders.

Many Americans do not like politics. This is understandable with all its underhanded back-room dealings, along with the questionable integrity of many who participate in it. And because so many people do not like politics, the best of us generally do not go into that field. The best of us usually pursue careers and live in a world of meritocracy, trying to do the best we can to make the organizations we are part of better off when we leave than when we first entered them.

This strong work ethic combined with a commitment to excellence is far from the "everyone needs to achieve mediocrity" the left emphasizes, and leftist leaders today are spreading a message of doom and gloom, without question. This vision is wrong. This vision is not the American way of hope and the 'can do attitude' that built this country!

We have lawmakers who are ruling against the will of the people. So, we need better leaders, we need leaders of much better character than we have now. We need leaders with integrity who have a high view of the Constitution and the Declaration of Independence, who will uphold the law by making sure it is applied equally and view the United States as the great nation it is. Thinking like this is crucial because when America falters, it ripples and cascades throughout the rest of the world and interactions between many countries go poorly. Replacing poor leaders with much better ones is essential.

America needs to regain its leadership position in the world as well. The United States needs to hold in check those countries that would be aggressors, and should apply pressure to dictators who attempt to impose their will on other countries. We need to return to being America, "a beacon of liberty,"[178] of brave, proud and free citizens. And to do this, we need to begin by regaining control of our borders.

The United States became a nation by defeating the strongest military power in the world at the time of our independence, namely Great Britain. Since that time, we have fought to keep this nation free and secure until now. Under our current leaders who do not care that their actions are hurting U.S. citizens, the U.S. government is turning a blind eye and not enforcing our sovereignty and allowing people to come into our country that have no regard for our laws. Those entering illegally have no regard for laws that state how to properly enter our country, so why would they care to obey the law once they are inside of the country?

If the country is as bad and racist as the leftists claim, why is the United States the number one destination for all the many minorities in the world who want to immigrate?[179] It is the number one destination because it is the greatest country on the face of the earth! Those who want to immigrate know this, yet our Democrat leftist political leaders either pretend they do not or actually do not.

In short, to start solving these difficult and complex problems, we must first replace the current poor leaders, then demand that the Constitution be enforced. Next, we protect families by supporting parents and stop those trying to undermine their authority over their children. We also must quickly regain energy independence on the way to becoming energy dominant. Safety is a priority on my list, which means we need to rebuild our military and focus on improving our cities by making them safe places to live. Securing our borders is linked to safety and reducing crime, so shutting down the flow of illegal aliens is all-important. Last but not least, we need to make monetary policy such that we only pay for what we can afford and not print money for things that are not necessary for us to prosper as a nation. These are my suggestions for what we do to get America back on track.

# FINAL THOUGHTS

In this Memoir, I shared some stories of how I grew up both in the United States and overseas to show a perspective developed from a wealth of personal experiences. As a Black American, I encountered some racial issues like what many Black Americans have experienced. But these examples do not mean that the United States is a racist nation. Nigerian immigrants performing the best of immigrants from any nation and minorities coming by the millions at great personal risk to enter the United States by any means they can confirms this point.

**So what? The answer is clear: we need better leaders.**

I have lived the American Dream. The Democrats want to take that opportunity away from all Americans by transforming the United States into another failed Marxist State through imposing their socialist policies on us. The steady decline all around this great country is a wake-up call. It is time to vote the career politicians out of office, along with those who have gone along with them, and replace these people with better leaders.

Sadly, the present politicians have brought the United States to the low point we are in today. We need to elect leaders who have high integrity, strength of character, and who have done something with their lives—not leaders like those in office now who participated in causing the steady decline of the United States where citizens suffer while politicians become richer every year. We need better leaders, and we need them now.

It is in your hands to make this happen. On November 19, 1863, President Abraham Lincoln in his Gettysburg Address said, "…that government of the people, by the people, for the people, shall not perish from the earth." Get engaged, become informed, and then stay informed. Most important though, take action by exercising your Constitutional right to vote, a precious right kept possible by the ultimate sacrifice of many in uniform.

**The choice is yours.**

# APPENDIX

# TONY GRADY

The award to the Cadet Who Best Exemplifies the Highest Ideals of Loyalty, Integrity, and Courage, sponsored by Family and Friends of Major General John K. Hester in His Memory, presented by Mrs. Virginia Hester Wooddell, daughter of General Hester, to Cadet Walter A. Grady Jr., 21st Squadron on May 30, 1977, at the United States Air Force Academy.

My parents at my individual award ceremony on May 30, 1977, the day before I graduated from the United States Air Force Academy. From left to right: Walter A, Grady Sr., Virginia Hester Woodall, Walter A. Grady Jr., Dorothy H. Grady.

154

# AMERICAN VALUES: ANOTHER VOICE

**DEPARTMENT OF THE AIR FORCE**
HEADQUARTERS 412TH TEST WING (AFMC)
EDWARDS AIR FORCE BASE, CALIFORNIA

412TG/CC
120 East Jones Road
Edwards AFB CA 93524-8290

21 Mar 97

To Whom It May Concern: (Letter of Recommendation, Lt Col Walter A. "Tony" Grady, Jr.)

This one is easy. *I give my highest recommendation for Lt Col Walter A. Grady, Jr.* There is not a finer professional aviator, officer, or gentleman that I have known. Tony brings a unique strength of leadership, moral character, and understanding to the table. This stands him apart from any of his peers.

I have now commanded two selectively manned flying organizations. In each, I was able to hand-pick those aviators and professionals in whom I would entrust the safety of this nation's leaders and its most valuable warfighting resources. The first was charged with the world-wide special airlift of the Air Force's senior leadership. The second was responsible for the test and evaluation of America's newest weapon of peace, the B-2. All of those aviators and professionals have gone to greater accomplishments--certified war heroes, recognized acquisition leaders, special air mission and airline standouts. I recommended them all--but Tony comes with my highest recommendation, yet. He's a sure-fire selection.

Let me tell you about Lt Col Grady. An Air Force Academy graduate, Tony has lived and practiced the virtue, morals, and ethics that make that institution one of this nation's finest. For Tony, living large is a matter of the heart, as well as of the mind. *That's important, because you can trust in Tony.* His flying record is incomparable...you'll see that in his professional and flying evaluations and records. *That's important, because experience is the best teacher.* He cares for the people I have asked him to command. More than any other I have had work for me, Tony works at being a leader. *That's important, because he'll do the same for you.*

I'm a Tony Grady fan--you can see that. I am confident you'll soon become a fan, too. Lt Col Tony Grady will make an excellent addition to your organization.

Sincerely

STUART L. HAUPT, Colonel, USAF
Director, B-2 Combined Test Force

Recommendation written by Col. Stuart L. Haupt,
B-2 Combined Test Force Director for Lt. Col. Tony Grady.

# TONY GRADY

> To the Eagle Board of Review
>
> and Far East Council Executives
>
> Dear Fellow Scouters:
>
> I am very happy to have this opportunity to recommend Walter A. Grady, Jr., better known to us in Bangkok as Tony, for the rank of Eagle Scout.
>
> Each letter of recommendation you receive, I am sure, will attest to the cheerful and high moral character of this fine lad; I certainly endorse those recommendations.
>
> Perhaps no one in scouting has been able to more closely observe him than his Scoutmaster - and all that I've witnessed for almost two years on the many meetings and campouts throughout Thailand, in Japan, and in Malaysia, have confirmed my opinion that Tony deserves Scouting's highest rank. Time after time he has demonstrated his ability to lead, and to follow willingly the advice of adult leaders, always in a most friendly manner.
>
> His unique Eagle project is a manifestation of his deep interest in the brotherhood of mankind.
>
> An Eagle is a rare Scout, exemplifying all we in the audience believe is the ultimate good in human nature and responsible leadership. Tony Grady belongs in that select group.
>
> Sincerely Yours in Scouting,
>
> Preston E. Law, Jr.
> Scoutmaster, Troop 702 Bangkok

Eagle Scout Award recommendation letter written by my Scoutmaster, Preston Law. This letter was written in 1971.

# AMERICAN VALUES: ANOTHER VOICE

*4/28/71*

*Dear Mrs. Gably —*

*I have enclosed a copy of the recommendation I wrote for Tony. It might embarrass him to know I think so highly of him! And I see by other letters I'm by no means alone in my opinion. I'm sure you are very proud of him.*

*So you might know how seldom I have the occasion to recommend a boy for Eagle, Tony is just my 4th in the nearly 6 years I've been a Scoutmaster — can you imagine how many hundreds of Boy Scouts I've had in my troops since 1965? Yet I knew Tony had what it takes the first time I met him at our meeting.*

*This is only the beginning of the honor he'll be bringing his mother, I'm sure.*

*Best Regards,*
*Rex Law*

Note to my mother that Scoutmaster Law attached to my Eagle Scout Recommendation letter. I was only the fourth boy that he recommended for the rank of Eagle Scout. Becoming and Eagle Scout was a major accomplishment for me, and I was very proud to wear the Eagle Scout Rank. This note was written in Bangkok, Thailand in 1971.

The Scoutmaster Award of Merit was given to Tony Grady
after he served as Scoutmaster from 2005-2009, for Troop 71,
sponsored by Aley United Methodist Church, Beavercreek, OH.

AMERICAN VALUES: ANOTHER VOICE

My sister Walteen Truely and me on May 30, 1977, the day before I graduated from the United States Air Force Academy.

A birthday celebration with our four children.

The Grady children at Whiting Field, in Pensacola, Florida, where John received his Naval Aviator Wings, on March 19, 2011. From left to right: Jasmine, Benjamin, John, and Holly. John is an Annapolis graduate. In this photo Benjamin is a Pleeb or Freshman at West Point. Though classes were in session, because his brother's winging ceremony was an official military formation, West Point allowed Benjamin to travel to Florida to attend this event.

AMERICAN VALUES: ANOTHER VOICE

The family at our daughter Jasmine's wedding. From left to right: back row: Benjamin, John; front row, Tony, Donna, Jasmine, and Holly.

TONY GRADY

# The seven classes of the National Championship Reno Air Races

STOL Drag Class

Sport Class

AMERICAN VALUES: ANOTHER VOICE

Unlimited Class

Formula One Class

# TONY GRADY

Jet Class

Biplane Class

# AMERICAN VALUES: ANOTHER VOICE

T-6 Class

Northrop-Grumman's B-2 Stealth Bomber test aircraft landing at Edwards Air Force Base, California in 1994. Tony Grady commanded the 420th Flight Test Squadron, located at Edwards Air Force Base from 1996 to 1997. This squadron verified that the B-2 met the design requirements specified by the United States Air Force.

Tony Grady standing in front of an F-16A at Edwards Air Force Base in May 1997. The aircraft was used for chase operations during B-2 Test Flights. Most of the 420th Squadron Test Pilots flew the F-16.

# AMERICAN VALUES: ANOTHER VOICE

# ENDNOTES

1. Tony Grady was one of twenty authors who contributed, writing Chapter 17, The Two Keys to Making a Better World: How-Do and Can-Do. The twenty authors dedicated this book to Mr. Philip A. Reeves their high school biology teacher and advisor to the Student Science Society of the International School Bangkok, Thailand.
2. He also wrote *Johnathan Livingston Seagull*.
3. Larry Schweikart and Michael Allen. *A Patriot's History of the United States: From Columbus's Great Discovery to the War on Terror* (375 Hudson Street, New York, New York 10014, USA: Sentinel, Penguin Group (USA) Inc., 2004), 354, 355. The Reconstruction plan developed by the United States Government was never fully implemented.
4. Ibid.
5. Ibid.
6. Ibid.
7. At the end of the election day for the presidential election of 1876, no clear winner had emerged. A deal was subsequently struck that the Democrats would switch 20 electoral college votes from Samuel Tilden to Rutherford B. Hayes if in return Federal troops would be withdrawn from the South. The Southern Democrats had promised in the deal to protect both the civil and political rights of its Black population, but that promise was not kept, so the troop withdrawal effectively ended Reconstruction and instituted the system of Jim Crow.
8. John Hope Franklin, *From Slavery to Freedom: A History of Negro Americans*, Fifth Edition (201 East 50th Street, New York, N.Y 10022: Alfred A. Knopf, Inc., 1980), 238.
9. Franklin, *From Slavery to Freedom*, 266, 258-259.
10. Ibid., 259.
11. Schweikart, Allen, *A Patriot's History*, 355.

12  Much of the early historical information regarding my grandparents was taken from the family history written by my Uncle Gordon. He compiled this information to construct the family tree.
13  About Southern Pines History, https://southernpines.net/162/History.
14  Ibid.
15  Energy King 480K Manual: Banking allows a person to recharge in such a manner as to retain a hot coal bed throughout the night. Approximately one hour before retiring for the night, push the coals to the rear of the firebox with the coal tapered down in front. Add a new layer of coal. Always leave some hot coals exposed in the front. This allows more coal to be added to the firebox, and it burns off the volatiles that could later cause an explosion (buff back).
16  At the time, a new innovative method by which President Roosevelt communicated with the American people.
17  About Southern Pines History, https://southernpines.net/162/History.
18  Ibid.
19  Bill Case, *"The Legacy of Boyd House,"* PineStraw Magazine, December 31, 2021, https://pinestrawmag.com/the-legacy-of-boyd-house/.
20  Ibid.
21  Ibid.
22  Franklin, *From Slavery to Freedom,* 271-272.
23  David E. Wharton, *A Struggle Worthy Of Note: The Engineering and Technological Education of Black Americans* (Greenwood Press, 88 Post Road West, Westport, CT 06881: Greenwood Publishing Group, Inc., 1992), 83.
24  Ibid., 82.
25  Franklin, *From Slavery to Freedom,* 236.
26  Hampton University History, https://home.hamptonu.edu/about/history/.
27  Ibid.
28  Ibid.
29  Ibid.
30  Ibid.
31  Ibid.
32  Ibid.
33  Ibid.
34  Ibid.
35  Discover the History of Mooresville, NC, https://www.mooresvillenc150.com/history/.
36  Ibid.
37  Ibid.
38  Unfortunately, no information could be found to further identify this gracious couple.
39  Paul Robeson, *Here I Stand* (Boston, MA: Beacon Press Books, 1958. Preface by Lloyd L. Brown, 1971), ix.

40  "In 1881, Booker T. Washington arrived in Alabama and started building Tuskegee Institute both in reputation and literally brick by brick. He recruited the best and the brightest to come and teach here including George Washington Carver who arrived in 1896. Carver's innovations in agriculture, especially with peanuts, expanded Tuskegee's standing throughout the country." Tuskegee Institute National Historical Site, Alabama, March 4, 2020, https://www.nps.gov/tuin/index.htm
41  International Labour Organization, *"History of the ILO,"* https://www.ilo.org/global/about-the-ilo/history/lang--en/index.htm
42  Ibid.
43  Treaty of Versailles, Section I., Organization of Labour[sic], paragraph 2, April 11, 1919, 1.
44  USAID From The American People, USAID History, *"Celebrating Sixty Years of Progress,"* https://www.usaid.gov/about-us/usaid-history.
45  Ibid.
46  In addition to Edwards Air Force Base, there is Patuxent River Naval Air Station, operated by the U.S. Navy, located in St. Mary's County, Maryland, on the Chesapeake Bay. The British operate Boscombe Down located outside of Amesbury, Wiltshire, England, and there is a French school, École du personnel Navigant d'essais et de réception or EPNER, located on Istres Le Tube Airbase in France.
47  Not the actual name of the member.
48  Matthew 22:39 (English Standard Version of the Bible).
49  Robert Kovach, *"The other side of the student story,"* Bangkok Post, circa 1973.
50  See Mr. Law's Eagle Scout Recommendation letter in the Appendix, 157, 158.
51  See the Scoutmaster Award of Merit in the Appendix, 155.
52  A slide rule is a mechanical device with special scales used to solve engineering problems. The middle part can move or slide back and forth.
53  Air Force Biography, Major General John K. Hester, September 1964, https://www.af.mil/About-Us/Biographies/Display/Article/106745/major-general-john-k-hester/
54  A Heritage Channel Arsenal Memorial Day Video summarizing Major General Hester's Accomplishments, https://www.youtube.com/watch?v=4u7eD_fr2LI.
55  See a photographs of the presentation of this award in the Appendix, 154.
56  Thomas Newdick, *"A Look Back At All The B-52 Variants As The Iconic Bomber Hits 70,"* The Warzone, April 16, 2022, https://www.twz.com/a-look-back-at-all-the-b-52-variants-as-the-iconic-bomber-hits-70.
57  FedEx Corporation, Company-Histories.com, https://www.company-histories.com/FedEx-Corporation-Company-History.html.
58  Ahmad Sanusi Husain, *"Fred Smith, Founder of FedEx: From Grade "C" Paper to a Global Business,"* LinkedIn, February 4, 2017, https://www.linkedin.com/pulse/fred-smith-founder-fedex-from-grade-c-paper-global-business-husain/.

59  See Colonel's Haupt's recommendation letter in the Appendix, 155.
60  Red Flag is a simulated Air War to prepare pilots for air combat operations.
61  See photos of airplanes in each race class for the National Championship Reno Air Races in the Appendix, 162-165.
62  Peter Summerlin, *"Magnolia River Ranch,"* Residential Design Award Of Honor, American Society Of Landscape Architects, 2006, https://www.asla.org/awards/2006/studentawards/282.html.
63  Constitution, History, March 28, 2023, https://www.history.com/topics/united-states-constitution/constitution.
64  Schweikart, Allen, *A Patriot's History,* 662-663.
65  Becky Little, *"How Gerrymandering Began in the US."* History Classics, August 7, 2023, https://www.history.com/news/gerrymandering-origins-voting.
66  Alison Durkee, *"80% Of Americans Support Voter ID Rules—But Fewer Worried About Fraud, Poll Finds,"* Forbes, June 21, 2021, https://www.forbes.com/sites/alisondurkee/2021/06/21/80-of-americans-support-voter-id-rules-but-fewer-worried-about-fraud-poll-finds/?sh=1dd9a2116041.
67  Megan Barth, *"Poll: 74 percent of Nevadans Support Voter ID,"* The Nevada Globe, February 10, 2023, https://thenevadaglobe.com/articles/poll-74-percent-of-nevadans-support-voter-id/.
68  Anthony Hamilton, Millard Kirk-Greene, Toyin O. Falola, J.E. Luebering, *"Nigerian Civil War [1967-1970],"* Britannica, https://www.britannica.com/topic/Nigerian-civil-war.
69  Ibid.
70  China Mike, *"The Mao Years [1949-1976],"* April 21, 2020, https://www.china-mike.com/chinese-history-timeline/part-14-mao-zedong/.
71  Ibid.
72  Ibid.
73  Jennifer Rosenberg, *"Tet Offensive,"* ThoughtCo., August 17, 2018, https://www.thoughtco.com/tet-offensive-vietnam-1779378.
74  University of Minnesota, *"Cambodia,"* Holocaust and Genocide Studies, https://cla.umn.edu/chgs/holocaust-genocide-education/resource-guides/cambodia.
75  John Uri, *"60 Years Ago: John Glenn, the First American to Orbit the Earth aboard Friendship 7,"* Johnson Space Center, February 18, 2022, https://www.nasa.gov/history/60-years-ago-john-glenn-the-first-american-to-orbit-the-earth-aboard-friendship-7/.
76  John Adams. October 11, 1798, in a letter to the officers or the First Brigade of the Third Division of the Militia of Massachusetts. Cited in William J. Federer, *AMERICA'S GOD AND COUNTRY: Encyclopedia Of Quotations* (Coppell, Texas, FAME Publishing, Inc., 1994), 10.
77  John Adams. 1774, in a letter to his wife Abigail relating the events of the First Continental Congress. Cited in William J. Federer, *AMERICA'S GOD AND*

*COUNTRY: Encyclopedia Of Quotations*. (Coppell, Texas, FAME Publishing, Inc., 1994), 6, 7.
78  National Constitution Center Staff, *"The day the Constitution was ratified,"* June 21, 2023, https://constitutioncenter.org/blog/the-day-the-constitution-was-ratified.
79  The Messiah is an uplifting arrangement of songs composed by German composer George Frideric Handel with the words written by his good friend Charles Jennens a wealthy English landowner. This masterpiece puts to music the life of Jesus Christ. Since this musical composition is so long, during the Christmas season the part that related to the Crucifixion of Christ is not sung.
80  Dr. Robert W Spoede, *More Than Conquerors: A History Of the Officers' Christian Fellowship Of The U.S.A 1943 to 1983* (Englewood, Colorado, OCF Books, 1993), 13.
81  Betty Lee Skinner, *DAWS A Man Who Trusted God* (Colorado Springs, Colorado, NavPress Publishing Group, 1974), 31.
82  Navigators, *"History of The Navigators,"* https://www.navigators.org/about/history/.
83  History.com, *"Korean War,"* May 11, 2022, https://www.history.com/topics/asian-history/korean-war.
84  Sebastien Roblin, *"In 1983, North Korea Tried to Blow up South Korea's President,"* The National Interest, April 25, 2020, https://nationalinterest.org/blog/buzz/1983-north-korea-tried-blow-south-koreas-president-147871.
85  Not his real name.
86  Diptarka Ghosh, *"Commonwealth Of Independent States,"* World Facts, WorldAtlas, March 26, 2021, https://www.worldatlas.com/articles/commonwealth-of-independent-states.html.
87  Lewis Foster, *Selecting A Translation Of The Bible* (Cincinnati, Ohio: Standard publishing,1978), 18. John Wycliffe translated the first Bible into English in 1382.
88  Thomas Jefferson. January 1, 1802, in a personal letter to Nehemiah Dodge, Ephraim Robbins, and Stephen Nelson of the Danbury Baptist Association, Danbury Connecticut… cited in, William Je. Federer, *America's God And Country Encyclopedia of Quotations* (Coppell, Texas, FAME Publishing, Inc., 1994), 325.
89  David Gibbs, Jr. & David Gibbs III, *Understanding The Constitution: Ten Things Every Christian Should Know About The Supreme Law Of The Land* (Seminole, Florida, Christian Law Association, 2006), 27.
90  *The Continental Reformation: Germany, Switzerland, and France, Zwingli and his influence,* "The Anabaptists," Britannica, History & Society, https://www.britannica.com/topic/Protestantism/The-Anabaptists.
91  Schweikart, Allen, *A Patriot's History,* 97, 98.
92  Ibid., 98.

93 "Our History," The Institutes for the Achievement of Human Potential, https://iahp.org/history-of-the-institutes/.
94 Glenn Doman, What To Do About Your Brain-Injured Child (Garden City, New York: Doubleday & Company, Inc., 1974), 7.
95 Ibid., 31.
96 David Bowman, *"Symphony recital romantic,"* Sunday Montgomery Adviser, December 10, 1992, 28.
97 Ibid.
98 Sean Salai, "Bill Bennett launches online U.S. history curriculum to fight 'anti-America' bias," The Washington Times, October 4, 2021, https://www.washingtontimes.com/news/2021/oct/4/bill-bennett-launches-online-us-history-curriculum/.
99 Peter K. Underwood, Michael P. Harmon, Wing Commander Robert A. Mason, Capt. John F. Guilmartin, Capt. Jerry Brown, *Contrails, Volume 19, 1973-74: The Air Force Cadet Handbook* (Colorado Springs, Colorado: United States Air Force Academy, 1973), 173. Excerpt from the Oath of Allegiance to the United States.
100 Quote from, P. McCree Thornton, *The Star Spangled Son* (Infinity Publishing, January 1, 2011), https://www.goodreads.com/quotes/510559-to-those-who-have-fought-for-it-freedom-has-a.
101 In his 1948 book of the same name, American philosopher Richard M. Weaver popularized the phrase *"Ideas have consequences."* The ideal that ideas have practical ramifications, on the other hand, is considerably older and can be found in the writings of many philosophers throughout history, such as Aristotle, Plato, and Descartes. https://archive.org/details/richard-m-weaver-ideas-have-consequences.
102 "God is the Grantor of freedom," David Gibbs, Jr. & David Gibbs III, *Understanding The Constitution*, 4.
103 Ibid., 65.
104 Schweikart, Allen, *A Patriot's History*, 117.
105 Erik M. Jensen, "Three-fifths Clause, Article I, Section 2, Clause 3," The Heritage Guide to the Constitution, https://www.heritage.org/constitution/#!/articles/1/essays/6/three-fifths-clause.
106 This was an unfortunate compromise but thought necessary to keep the colonies unified to form a new nation. Compromise is at the center of the political process when opponents overcome a problem that they ardently disagree on. In reality, time marches on and the political body must respond. Inaction in some cases is not an option. In the case dealing with slavery, at the beginning of the United States, a passionate disagreement took place. Beyond the scope of this book, I would encourage the reader to look at slavery in context in the past especially during the period of the 1800s. It was prevalent throughout the entire world. I am not defending this heinous practice, but I am cautioning overlaying 21st century morals on a 19th century society. That

is not the proper way to study history in order to understand what happened in the past and possibly make inferences as to why. See, Schweikart, Allen, *A Patriot's History*, 116.

107 A right is something inherent to all people at all times throughout human existence. It does not depend on a specific time period in history. The Founders recognized this and wrote down what those rights were. Something does not become a right just because an individual or group thinks it should be a right. Rights come from God, the Creator.

108 David A. Noebel, *Understanding The Times: The Religious Worldviews of Our Day and the Search For Truth* (Manitou Springs, Colorado, Harvest House Publishers, 1991), 75.

109 Nicolle Yapur, *"Venezuela Breaks One of World's Longest Hyperinflation Bouts,"* Bloomberg, January 14, 2022, https://www.bloomberg.com/news/articles/2022-01-14/venezuela-breaks-one-of-worlds-longest-hyperinflation-bouts?leadSource=uverify%20wall.

110 *"One in three Venezuelans not getting enough to eat, UN study finds,"* United Nations, February 25, 2020, https://news.un.org/en/story/2020/02/1058051.

111 Noebel, Understanding The Times, 676-677.

112 Tom Tillison, *"Whole Foods CEO warns socialism is a failed system that 'impoverishes everything,' says colleges are the problem,"* BPR Business & Politics, November 27, 2020, https://www.bizpacreview.com/2020/11/27/whole-foods-ceo-warns-socialism-is-a-failed-system-that-impoverishes-everything-says-colleges-are-the-problem-1000130/.

113 David A. Noebel, Understanding The Times, 68.

114 Ibid., 520.

115 Ibid., 670-671, p. 748.

116 Ibid., 676.

117 Edgar Hardcastle, *"The Withering Away of the State—From Marx to Stalin,"* Socialist Standard, March 1946, https://www.marxists.org/archive/hardcastle/1946/wither_away.htm.

118 Bradley Thomas, *"Antonio Gramsci: the Godfather of Cultural Marxism,"* FEE Stories, March 31, 2019, https://fee.org/articles/antonio-gramsci-the-godfather-of-cultural-marxism/.

119 Ibid.

120 Lawrence W. Reed, *"Why the Pilgrims Abandoned Common Ownership for Private Property,"* FEE Stories, November 25, 2019, https://fee.org/articles/why-the-pilgrims-abandoned-common-ownership-for-private-property/.

121 Christopher F. Rufo, *"Critical Race Theory: What It Is and How to Fight It,"* Imprimis, A Publication Of Hillsdale College Volume 50, Number 3 (March 2021): 1. https://imprimis.hillsdale.edu/wp-content/uploads/2021/04/Imprimis_Mar_3-21_6pgNM.pdf.

122 Katharine Gorka and Mike Gonzalez, *"The Radicalization of Race: Philanthropy and DEI,"* The Heritage Foundation, Special Report No. 236,

(December 21, 2022) 19. https://www.heritage.org/sites/default/files/2022-12/SR263.pdf.
123 Rufo, *"Critical Race Theory,"* 3.
124 Gorka and Gonzalez, *"The Radicalization of Race,"* 19, 23.
125 Rufo, "Critical Race Theory", 2.
126 Ibid., 3.
127 Ibid., 3.
128 Ibid., 5.
129 Gorka and Gonzalez, *"The Radicalization of Race,"* 23.
130 Ibid., 26.
131 Michael Scheuer, *"The Democrats: The party of five infamous 'S's' adds a 'T' for treason,"* Michael Scheuer/Non-Intervention, December 11, 2010, https://www.non-intervention2.com/2010/12/11/the-democrats-the-party-of-five-infamous-ss-adds-a-t-for-treason/.
132 Paul Kengor, *"How Barak Obama Fundamentally Transformed the United States,"* National Catholic Register, January 12, 2017, https://www.ncregister.com/news/how-barack-obama-fundamentally-transformed-the-united-states.
133 Amanda Onion, Missy Sullivan, Matt Mullen, Christian Zapata, *"1854 Republican Party founded,"* History, February 9, 2010, https://www.history.com/this-day-in-history/republican-party-founded.
134 *"The Reconstruction Acts of 1867,"* History & Ourselves, https://www.facinghistory.org/resource-library/reconstruction-acts-1867.
135 Tom Head, "Timeline History of the Ku Klux Klan," ThoughtCo., December 13, 2020, https://www.thoughtco.com/the-ku-klux-klan-history-721444.
136 *"The Ku Klux Klan,"* National Geographic, https://education.nationalgeographic.org/resource/ku-klux-klan/.
137 Theodore Eisenberg, *"Civil Rights Repeal Act 28 Sat. 36 (1894),"* Encyclopedia.com, https://www.encyclopedia.com/politics/encyclopedias-almanacs-transcripts-and-maps/civil-rights-repeal-act-28-stat-36-1894.
138 *"Woodrow Wilson: Federal Segregation,"* Smithsonian National Postal Museum, https://postalmuseum.si.edu/research-articles/the-history-and-experience-of-african-americans-in-america's-postal-service-3.
139 Brian Burnes, *"Harry Truman's Remarkably Fraught First Political Campaign,"* FLATLAND, August 10, 2022, https://flatlandkc.org/arts-culture/harry-trumans-remarkably-fraught-first-political-campaign/.
140 George Wallace, *"Segregation Now, Segregation Tomorrow, Segregation Forever,"* wyzant, January 14, 1963, https://www.wyzant.com/resources/lessons/history/hpol/wallace/segregation/?url%20Name=&g=GoogleAdwords&awcampaignid=16555669629&awadgroupid=%20&awaceid=&awcid=&awim=&awkw=&awmt=&awn=x&awp=&awt=&mkwid=%20&pcrid=&pkw=&pmt=&pdv=c&slid=&physid=1024403&intid=&bgSeg=%20&gclid=EAIaIQobChMIl8jpqcSNgQMVDQGtBh04iAMMEAAYASAAEg%20INYvD_BwE.

141 *"Civil Rights Act (1964),"* National Archives, July 2, 1964, https://www.archives.gov/milestone-documents/civil-rights-act.

142 Dareh Gregorian and Hallie Jackson, *"Va. Gov. Northam's yearbook pic of men in blackface, Klan robe spurs calls for his resignation,"* NBC News, February 1, 2019, https://www.nbcnews.com/politics/politics-news/reports-virginia-governor-s-yearbook-page-had-photo-men-blackface-n966066.

143 Ciara O'Rourke, *"Robert Byrd wasn't a Grand Wizard of the KKK but he once led a local chapter,"* POLITIFACT, August 15, 2019, https://www.politifact.com/factchecks/2019/aug/15/viral-image/robert-byrd-wasnt-grand-wizard-kkk-he-once-led-loc/.

144 Tim Scott SLAMS Dick Durbin For Calling His Bill "Token" Legislation, BlazeTV, https://www.youtube.com/watch?v=vrakLL0pzLA.

145 Jennifer Agiesta, *"Most say race relations worsened under Obama, poll finds,"* CNN politics, October 5, 2016, https://www.cnn.com/2016/10/05/politics/obama-race-relations-poll/index.html.

146 There were 1,461 appointed or selected to attend the Air Force Academy on Monday, July 2, 1977. The numbers given are approximate and meant for illustration purposes.

147 Although I distinctly remember this conversation, in researching the policy, Col. Gail Colvin, USAF (Retired) informed me that this was not a formal policy, but that the Air Force Academy Vice Commandant, an assignment that she served in, made sure that cadets did not go into a squadron feeling isolated. She shared that she personally moved Basic Cadets to other squadrons at the end of Basic Cadet Training.

148 The Commandant's List signified military merit, as the Dean's List signifies academic merit.

149 Roland G. Fryer, Jr., *"An Empirical analysis of Racial Difference in Police Use of Force,"* July 2017, 4.

150 Ibid., 29.

151 According to NASA, https://www.nasa.gov/centers/dryden/aircraft/T-38/peformance.html.
https://www.af.mil/About-Us/Fact-Sheets/Display/Article/104569/t-38-talon/.

152 Schweikart, Allen, *A Patriot's History Of The United States,* xxiii.

153 "Afghanistan War," History, August 20, 2021, https://www.history.com/topics/21st-century/afghanistan-war.

154 Rebecca Kheel, *"Billions in US weaponry seized by Taliban,"* The Hill, August 19, 2021, https://thehill.com/policy/defense/568493-billions-in-us-weaponry-seized-by-taliban/?rl=1.

155 Jack Detsch, Kelly Kimball, and Robbie Gramer, *"State Department: Thousands of U.S. Residents Still Stuck in Afghanistan,"* Foreign Policy, November 3, 2021, https://foreignpolicy.com/2021/11/03/state-department-afghanistan-us-residents/.

156 Shoshana Bryen: *"China, Russia, And Iran Rush to Fill The American Leadership Void,"* Daily Caller, May 1, 2023, https://dailycaller.com/2023/05/01/opinion-china-russia-and-iran-rush-to-fill-the-american-leadership-void-shoshana-bryen/.

157 Raffi Berg, *"Iran and Saudi Arabia to renew ties after seven-year rift,"* BBC, March 10, 2023, https://www.bbc.com/news/world-middle-east-64906996.

158 Ibid.

159 *"China-Taiwan military tensions 'worst in 40 years',"* BBC, October 6, 2021, https://www.bbc.com/news/world-asia-58812100.

160 John Mac Ghlionn, *"China Now Controls Africa,"* THE EPOCH TIMES, December 23, 2021, https://www.theepochtimes.com/opinion/china-now-controls-africa-4165363.

161 James McBride, Noah Berman, and Andrew Chatzky, *"China's Massive Belt and Road Initiative,"* Council on Foreign Relations, February 2, 2023, https://www.cfr.org/backgrounder/chinas-massive-belt-and-road-initiative.

162 Ghlionn, *China Now Controls Africa*.

163 Peter Landers, *"Japan Breaks With U.S. Allies, Buys Russian Oil at Prices Above Cap,"* THE WALL STREET JOURNAL, April 2, 2023, https://www.wsj.com/articles/japan-breaks-with-u-s-allies-buys-russian-oil-at-prices-above-cap-1395accb.

164 Ibid.

165 Jerry Hendrix, *"THE AGE OF AMERICAN NAVAL DOMINANCE IS OVER,"* The Atlantic, March 13, 2023, https://www.theatlantic.com/magazine/archive/2023/04/us-navy-oceanic-trade-impact-russia-china/673090/.

166 Ibid.

167 Mark Thomas-Patterson, *"Containing Soviet Nuclear Fission: Senator Sam Nunn and Cooperative Threat Reduction,"* Emory Libraries Scholar Blog, October 23, 2023, https://scholarblogs.emory.edu/marbl/2023/10/23/nunn/.

168 James K. Glassman, *"Moynihan's Social Security Plan,"* AEI American Enterprise Institute, March 24, 1998, https://www.aei.org/articles/moynihans-social-security-plan/.

169 Maggie Racki, *"ISW Awards Senator Joseph Lieberman For National Security Leadership,"* ISW Institute For The STUDY OF WAR, November 20, 2021, https://www.understandingwar.org/press-media/pressrelease/isw-awards-senator-joseph-lieberman-national-security-leadership.

170 Daniel Jativa, *"Rudy Giuliani: 'Rabid Democrats have 'no regard for the Constitution of the laws',"* Washington Examiner, April 4, 2019, https://www.washingtonexaminer.com/?p=1391080.

171 The Detox Center LA, *"Fentanyl is Now the Leading Cause of Death for American Adults, The Detox Center of Los Angeles is on the Front Lines,"* yahoo!finance, September 16, 2022, https://finance.yahoo.com/news/

fentanyl-now-leading-cause-death-211900029.html?guccounter=1&guce_referrer=aHR0cHM6Ly9kdWNr.

172 Corrie Pelc, *"New York state of emergency: Why polio has reemerged, and hos to stay safe,"* Medical News Today, September 12, 2022, https://www.medicalnewstoday.com/articles/why-polio-has-reemerged-and-how-to-stay-safe-experts-advise.

173 E McCray, C M Weinbaum, C R Braden, M Onorato, *"The epidemiology of tuberculosis in the United States,"* NIH National Library of Medicine March 18, 1997, https://pubmed.ncbi.nlm.nih.gov/9098614/.

174 Tristan justice, *"Left-Wing Martha's Vineyard Elites Deport Illegal Immigrants After Just 24 Hours,"* The Federalists, September 16, 2022, https://thefederalist.com/2022/09/16/left-wing-marthas-vineyard-elites-deport-illegal-immigrants-after-just-24-hours/.

175 Paul Wiseman, *"US economic growth for the last quarter is revised down to a 2.1% annual rate,"* AP, August 30, 2023, https://apnews.com/article/economy-gdp-inflation-federal-reserve-jobs-growth-8934ebcac23acdfef69089db2942f6d6.

176 Todd L. Pittinsky, *"Inflation Disproportionately Hurts the Poor,"* WSJ OPINION, June 20, 2021, https://www.wsj.com/articles/inflation-disproportionately-hurts-the-poor-11624207206.

177 Jenin Younes, *"Lockdowns Worsen the Health Crisis,"* AIER AMERICAN INSTITUTE for ECONOMIC RESEARCH, March 27, 2021, https://www.aier.org/article/lockdowns-worsen-the-health-crisis/.

178 Schweikart, Allen, *A Patriot's History Of The United States,* xxiii.

179 Betsy Reed, *"US is still the world's leading destination for immigrants,"* The Guardian, December 14, 2010, https://www.theguardian.com/world/2010/dec/14/united-states-immigration-numbers-perucca.

# BIOGRAPHY OF LIEUTENANT COLONEL WALTER A. "TONY" GRADY, JR., USAF RETIRED

Lieutenant Colonel Tony Grady was born December 5, 1955, in Norfolk, Virginia. He attended high school at the International School, Bangkok, Thailand where he participated in sports and was Sophomore, Junior, and Senior Class president. He graduated in 1973 and was appointed to the United States Air Force Academy. In 1977 he graduated from the United States Air Force Academy with a Bachelor of Science degree in Astronautical Engineering. Upon graduation he was distinguished as "The Cadet Who Best Exemplifies The Highest Ideals of Loyalty, Integrity and Courage" in the Class of 1977. He holds a Master of Science degree in Systems Management from the University of Southern California, and a Master of Airpower Art and Science from the Air University. He is also a graduate of The United States Air Force Test Pilot School, Air Command and Staff College, and the Defense Systems Management College.

Commissioned through the United States Air Force Academy, Colorado Springs, Colorado, Tony entered undergraduate pilot training at Williams Air Force Base, Arizona, in June 1977. His first operational assignment in 1978 was in the B-52D at the 7th Bombardment Wing, Carswell Air Force Base, Texas. In 1981 he was assigned as a Forward Air Controller to the 19th Tactical Air Support Squadron, Osan Air Base, Republic of Korea. There he flew first the OV-10A and then transitioned to the A-37B. He served as the wing and squadron scheduling and training officer, and aircraft maintenance evaluation pilot.

In 1984 Tony returned to the United States and was assigned to the 529th Bomb Squadron, 380th Bomb Wing, Plattsburgh Air Force Base, New York where he served as an FB-111 Flight Commander and Evaluator Instructor Pilot. He was also the 8th Air Force Nominee for the Jabara Award, given to the United States Air Force Academy graduate whose airmanship contributions are of great significance and set him apart from his contemporaries. In 1988 he attended the United States Air Force Test Pilot School at Edwards Air Force Base, California. Upon graduation he was assigned to the 4953rd Test Squadron, 4950th Test Wing, Wright-Patterson Air Force Base, Dayton, Ohio. Serving as the Combined Test Team Director and head test pilot for the T-1A Jayhawk, Tony led his team from source selection through first flight. In 1991 he attended Air Command and Staff College, Maxwell Air Force Base, Montgomery, Alabama. After graduation he was selected to attend the second class of the School of Advanced Airpower Studies, redesignated the School of Advanced Air & Space Studies in 2002, also at Maxwell Air Force Base.

After graduation from the School of Advanced Airpower Studies, Tony served on the Air Staff as the Long-Range Attack Team Chief of the Combat Forces Division, at the Pentagon where he planned and programmed all Air Force bomber forces. In 1994 he attended the Program Manager's course at the Defense Systems Management College, Fort Belvoir, Virginia. In 1995 he was assigned to the 420th Test Squadron, Edwards Air Force Base, California. The 420th was solely responsible for the successful test and evaluation of the B-2 stealth Bomber. He flew several first flights in the development of the B-2 Bomber, including the first night terrain following mission. He commanded the 420th Test Squadron from 1996 through 1997 when he retired from active military service.

## AMERICAN VALUES: ANOTHER VOICE

Tony Grady is a command pilot and an experienced test pilot with over 5,000 flying hours, in 47 different aircraft. His military decorations include the: Air Force Achievement Medal, Air Force Commendation Medal, Meritorious Service Medal, National Defense Service Medal, Combat Readiness Medal, Air Force Outstanding Unit Award, and Aerial Achievement Medal.

Tony was hired by FedEx in Nov 97 and retired in Dec 2017 as a MD-11 Captain. While at FedEx he served as an Instructor and a Line Check Airman. He also flew as a DC-10 Second Officer, an A-300 Airbus and MD-11 First Officer. During this time period, he flew out of Memphis, Tennessee; Subic Bay, Philippines; and Anchorage, Alaska.

In 2000 Tony founded and served for eleven years as CEO of Synerbotics a start-up biotechnology firm with the objective of designing and developing advanced medical devices by leveraging nanotechnology with biotechnology. Synerbotics offered problem solving research and development services to customers in the non-invasive surgical community. Synerbotics was a Phase 1 winner in the i-Zone 2002 Business Plan Competition in Dayton, Ohio. Synerbotics had discussions with the Cleveland Clinic Foundation for a possible partnering relationship.

An international speaker, Tony delivered an inspiration talk on pursing your goals, titled, 'Grasp Your Vision,' to the 2019 Portugal Air Summit held in Ponte de Sor, Portugal.

In 2021 Tony Served as the Director of Flight Operations/Race Director for the National Championship Reno Air Races. It was a resounding success after a one-year delay due to the COVID-19 Pandemic.

Tony was a 2022 Nevada Lieutenant Governor Republican Primary Candidate, winning thirteen of the seventeen Nevada Counties, and finishing second by 5.8%. Though a first-time candidate, he achieved statewide name recognition.

Tony is married to the former Donna Lynn Sweet of Burlington, Iowa. They have four children. All are college graduates. One graduated from Annapolis and another graduated from West Point.

# PHOTOS AND ILLUSTRATIONS

1. Eagle and Fledglings Statue in the Air Gardens at the U. S. Air Force Academy. (Grady Family Collection)
2. Walter Grady Sr. and Viola Grady at his graduation from Hampton Institute, January 19, 1944. (Grady Family Collection)
3. Walter Grady Sr. and Dorothy Grady in their house in Philadelphia in 1986. (Grady Family Collection)
4. Gordon Grady in Salem, Massachusetts on his ninetieth birthday in 2007. (Grady Family Collection)
5. 1977 United States Air Force Academy Recruiting Brochure. (U.S. government pamphlet)
6. John Grady on the monkey bars in 1987, in base housing at Plattsburgh Air Force Base, New York. (Grady Family Collection)
7. John and Jasmine Grady on the monkey bars in 1981, at home in Dayton, Ohio. (Grady Family Collection)
8. Tony Grady receiving the General Hester Award on May 30, 1977, at the U.S. Air Force Academy. (Grady Family Collection)
9. Walter and Dorothy Grady with Tony Grady holding the Eagle and Fledglings, May 30, 1977. (Grady Family Collection)
10. Letter of recommendation written by Colonel Stuart Haupt, Mar 21, 1997.
11. Eagle Scout Award recommendation letter.
12. Note accompanying Eagle Scout award recommendation letter, April 28, 1971.
13. Scoutmaster Award of Merit.

14. Tony and Walteen Grady on May 30, 1977, at the U.S. Air Force Academy. (Grady Family Collection)
15. Birthday celebration with the four Grady children. (Grady Family Collection)
16. John Grady received his Naval Aviator wings with his sisters and brother on March 19, 2011, in Pensacola, Florida. (Grady Family Collection)
17. The Grady Family at Jasmine's marriage ceremony. (Grady Family Collection)
18. Reno Air Race STOL/Drag Class airplane. (Reno Air Race Association photo used by permission)
19. Reno Air Race Sport Class airplane. (Reno Air Race Association photo used by permission)
20. Reno Air Race Unlimited Class airplane. (Unlimited class photo used by permission)
21. Reno Air Race Formula One Class airplane. (Reno Air Race Association photo used by permission)
22. Reno Air Race Jet Class airplane. (Reno Air Race Association photo used by permission)
23. Reno Air Race Biplane Class airplane. (Reno Air Race Association photo used by permission)
24. Reno Air Race T-6 Class airplane. (T-6 Class photo used by permission)
25. B-2 Stealth Bomber landing at Edwards Air Force Base. (Official Air Force photo used by permission)
26. Tony Grady standing in front of an F-16A at Edwards Air Force Base, California in May 1997. (Official Air Force photo used by permission)
27. Tony Grady on the flightline at Edwards Air Force Base, California. (Official Air Force photo used by permission)
28. Tony Grady official campaign photograph. (Courtesy of Lou Manna, Grady Family Collection)

Made in the USA
Las Vegas, NV
11 May 2024